The architecture of Ulrich Franzen

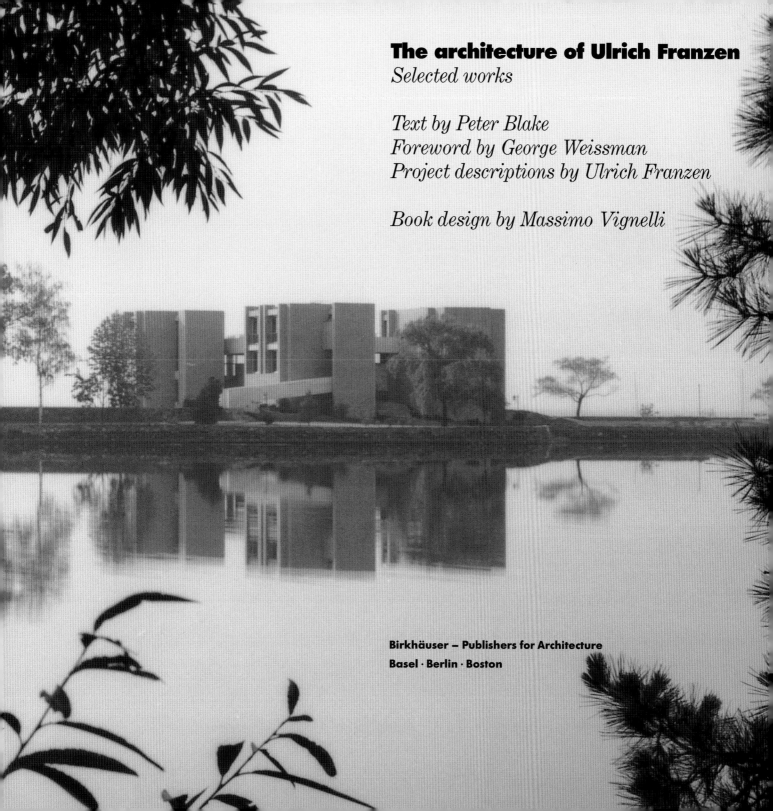

The architecture of Ulrich Franzen
Selected works

Text by Peter Blake
Foreword by George Weissman
Project descriptions by Ulrich Franzen

Book design by Massimo Vignelli

Birkhäuser – Publishers for Architecture
Basel · Berlin · Boston

Grateful appreciation is expressed to George Weissman, former Chairman of Lincoln Center for the Performing Arts, New York, for his kindness in introducing this publication with a foreword.

A CIP catalogue record for this book is available from the Library of Congress, Washington D. C., USA

Deutsche Bibliothek Cataloging-in-Publication Data

Blake, Peter:
The architcture of Ulrich Franzen / Peter Blake. - Basel ; Berlin ;
Boston : Birkhäuser, 1999
   ISBN 3-7643-5905-6 (Basel…)
   ISBN 0-8176-5905-6 (Boston)

© 1999 Birkhäuser – Publishers for Architecture, P. O. Box 133, CH-4010 Basel, Switzerland

The photographs and drawings were provided by the architect. The photographers are indicated on page 5.

Printed on acid-free paper produced from chlorine-free pulp
Printed in Germany
ISBN 3-7643-5905-6
ISBN 0-8176-5905-6

9 8 7 6 5 4 3 2 1

I have known Ulrich Franzen for more than forty years. Our relationship grew from client to friend to admirer.

In the course of this relationship, my view of architecture grew to where I now place it – at the highest level of visual experience. It is the art form that we live with during our waking hours. It assaults or pleases the eye. It creates the environment that enables us to function.

It is for all these qualities that I admire Rick.

I first met Rick in 1955. We had previously lived in a colonial home and this was demolished to make room for the New England Thruway. So we purchased a two-acre plot a mile away, in Rye, New York.

When I asked Ezra Stoller, the noted architectural photographer, to recommend a young architect who could build an "interesting" house for myself, my wife, and our three children, he suggested Rick.

For the next year, Rick was at our home, analyzing and psychoanalyzing how we lived, moved and functioned. As he designed our house, he consulted and *listened!* Although he had his own fixed ideas, he was resilient and responsive. And he would come up with a solution that met our needs and his aesthetics.

The result was a house beautiful. Through the use of large glass windows and clerestories throughout the structure, the outdoors came indoors. There was never a dull day. The house functioned well. It inspired my son to become an architect.

As a result of my personal experience, I then introduced Rick to the president of the Philip Morris Company, where I was a vice president. His first assignment was to redesign the 40,000 square foot executive floor at 100 Park Avenue in New York City.

Utilizing warm woods, lush carpets, clerestories and modern art, he designed an environment that was creative and reflected the spirit of a people-oriented office that was open and yet afforded privacy. A remarkable and totally unexpected aspect of the reconstruction was the manner in which the employees improved their dress and grooming to live up to the new environment.

In each of the projects that followed for Philip Morris, Rick did the exterior and interior designs. He introduced the company to the use of contemporary art and sculpture as a significant force to inspire creativity and to tell our employees that "we are open to new ideas and to new ways of looking at our business." The timing was fortunate. Rick's approach was an influential factor in generating Philip Morris's corporate support of the visual and performing arts.

His world headquarters for Philip Morris at 42nd Street and Park Avenue in Manhattan is a classic. When the Whitney opened its branch museum and sculpture garden, John Chamberlain proclaimed the space a "golden room."

Rick has a unique ability to create beautiful forms and aesthetic environments wherein the spaces and places enable people to work and live efficiently, pleasantly and comfortably.

If the word "classic" means enduring beauty, then Rick is the classic contemporary architect.

George Weissman

Here are the facts: Ulrich Franzen was born in 1921 in Düsseldorf, in the Rhineland. His family were writers and artists; and after Hitler came to power they decided to leave Germany and move to the United States. Franzen, after finishing high school, got a scholarship to Williams College, an admirable private institution in Massachusetts, where he became fascinated with art history, especially Romanesque and modern architecture.

After graduating from Williams, he served in U.S. Army Intelligence, and, after World War II, enrolled at Harvard's Graduate School of Design, then still dominated primarily by Walter Gropius and Marcel Breuer. Among his fellow students were Paul Rudolph, Philip Johnson, Harry Cobb, and John Johansen while Philip Johnson was a school mate and I. M. Pei a teacher. There were other fellow students who became significant second or third generation modernists in the postwar years as, of course, did Franzen. After graduating from Harvard, Franzen and Cobb went to work for I. M. Pei, in New York City. Pei had become an in-house architect for the developer William Zeckendorf, and much of the work in the Pei office tended to be exploratory; but now and then a project would be realized, and Franzen worked on one of those, the Mile High Center in Denver, a complex clearly influenced by Mies van der Rohe's high-rise apartments on Lake Shore Drive, in Chicago. Each time he went to Denver, he would stop off in Chicago on the way and look at Mies van der Rohe's buildings. On one of these occasions he met Mies, and was greatly impressed.

By 1955, Franzen had enough self-confidence (and one or two residential commissions) to leave Pei's office and establish his own practice. Pei, Cobb, and Franzen have remained friends, but Franzen was anxious to try to make it on his own. He succeeded, and became one of the most creative American architects in the second half of the twentieth century.

Unlike others of his generation, Franzen did not align his work with that of major role models of the first half of the century. Instead, he responded freely to numerous problems and opportunities in ways that were unorthodox and often singularly creative: he saw that each architectural problem tended to call for its own solution rather than for a "typical" plan or form; he saw that there were resources outside the conventional fields of architecture that offered ideas that could generate interesting images; he absorbed significant notions generated by avant-garde artists in other fields, and drew upon such notions in finding solutions not generally found in the work of his contemporaries; and he often questioned accepted standards of modern architecture and enriched his buildings in the process.

This book is an attempt to show what Ulrich Franzen did in the decades after he established his own practice, and what he was able to contribute to the theory, practice, and to the scope of modern architecture in that time.

Chapter 1

Architecture, toward the end of the twentieth century and in many parts of the world, had really ceased to be an art and become a business. Buildings, or the identifiable character or style of building, had become marketable products. Those familiar with the period can easily recognize who designed what: if a building was all white-on-white, you knew that it must be the work of Architect A; if a building was a compilation of squares upon squares upon squares, then it was the work of Architect B; if a building was an amorphous assemblage of curvaceous forms, it was very likely to be the work of Architect C; and if it consisted of dysfunctional angles, unhinged verticals as well as horizontals, it was clearly the latest work of Architect D. And so on.

It was, of course, slightly unsettling to find that buildings had become so stylized. After all, there is really no good reason why two buildings, even two buildings by the same architect, should be anything but superficially alike. The truth is that every building is, or should be, shaped by specific factors, no two of which are likely to be identical: there is, first of all, the site; next, in no particular order, the program, the context, the client, the materials used, the views, the time and, of course, the budget. No two or three or four of these factors are ever likely to be the same; and buildings shaped by all those factors cannot or should not be identical or even very similar.

There is, naturally, one constant: the architect's preferences. But even these may be shaped by many changing concerns.

Among the architects who have significantly shaped the second half of the twentieth century, Ulrich Franzen may be one of those most responsive to all the different factors that should influence each architect's work. Unlike some of his contemporaries mentioned earlier, Franzen has designed a great range and variety of buildings that vary considerably from each other in any number of respects, and respond to specific requirements in different and unexpected ways.

He is fond of talking about "collage" as a constant quality in his work; and collage, the assemblage of divergent qualities and characteristics seems about as good a way of describing his work as any. "Because so many different factors shape our buildings it seems inappropriate that the buildings should end up looking alike", he once said. And so it is not surprising that a collection of his buildings, over the past 40 or 50 years, should reveal a wide variety of forms and of details, in response to a wide variety of totally different factors. He is one of the most accomplished designers of "collage architecture" in our time.

Needless to say, one of the particularly important influences on his work has been the example of some of the principal "form givers" in architecture who have significantly influenced virtually every member of Franzen's generation. Not long ago, he came across a description of Alvar Aalto's work that clearly appealed to him. Marja-Ritta Norri, the Director of the Museum of Finnish Architecture, had written that Aalto "believed that the 'simultaneous solution of opposites' was the first necessary condition for a building or any human achievement to attain the level of culture."

Although Franzen, like others of his generation, was clearly aware of and impressed by Aalto's work, and by Aalto's ability to resolve opposites simultaneously, he was more impressed, at the beginning of his career, by the single-minded work of Mies van der Rohe, who had established himself in Chicago at about the same time that saw the establishment of the Harvard Graduate School of Design under Gropius and Breuer. Franzen remembers vividly that, in the years when he worked in Pei's office, everyone there would talk about Mies van der Rohe's work, and explore the beautiful details of his steel-and-glass buildings that were going up in Chicago. But Mies, Gropius, and Breuer were not the only ones who influenced Franzen and his generation; there was also Le Corbusier, whose work Franzen knew primarily through publications, and who was spending some time in New York during the years when the U. N. Headquarters were being planned; and there was Aalto, whose "binary" dormitory building for the Massachusetts Institute of Technology, with its two contradictory facades, seemed to violate much of what modern architects held sacred.

Still, it was Mies van der Rohe, above all others, whose work clearly influenced Franzen in many ways. And it was Mies van der Rohe's dictum that "God is in the Details" that stuck in Franzen's mind – though he preferred to say that "Architecture is in the Details." That conviction, more than any other, shaped Franzen's work throughout his career. That, and the need to find "simultaneous solutions of opposites."

But during the first several years of his independent career as an architect, Mies van der Rohe's compositions and details dominated Franzen's work. Like most young architects, just starting out on their own, he tended to attract clients who wanted houses designed for them; and Franzen's first houses, built in the 1950s and 1960s, were Miesian in general composition and in some detail, but quite free in specifics, not at all rigidly adherent to Mies's prototypes. They were, in fact, remarkably independent in almost every way, and Miesian only in spirit. The first of those houses, one he designed and built for himself and his first wife and their children in the late 1950s in Rye, New York, continues to be one of the finest modern houses built in the U. S. in the postwar years.

Unlike a number of young architects who were enamored with Mies van der Rohe's vocabulary and designed and built steel-and-glass houses similar to Mies's prototypes, Franzen's houses were special in that they related in general to Mies's work, but were distinctly different in detail and in overall composition: Mies van der Rohe's houses and other small structures tended to adhere to a rectangular geometry and often seemed almost classical in composition, while Franzen's houses were minimalist, high-tech, often triangulated, and always very delicate in detail. Unlike Philip Johnson's houses, which were orthodoxly Miesian and usually steel-framed with massive corner columns and roof beams, Franzen's houses were framed with triangulated trusses of very light steel, with corners of mitered sheets of glass and roof structures that seemed to float, almost literally, above the glass-enclosed living spaces. They seemed much more spare in their delicacy and lightness than the somewhat overdesigned structures that Mies van der Rohe's more orthodox disciples tended to prefer. In short, Franzen's houses were extraordinarily "modern" in their minimalist frames.

Yet, in their composition and in their open plans, they were entirely in keeping with Miesian prototypes admired by all of us in those days and admired still. The plans were open, sometimes almost too open for privacy, and the divisions and separations of the interior spaces were as minimalist as the supporting structure. Moreover, the houses tended to be pavilions placed on stone platforms that extended glass-walled interior spaces into the landscape.

What made those houses so fascinating to many of us was their maturity. These did not seem to be the first houses done by a young architect barely out of school. They were polished in their detailing, and self-assured in their composition. Nothing seemed to have been left to chance; everything was in place, and properly joined to everything else. Not bad for the first independent efforts by a relatively new talent.

The detailing was especially impressive: in all of his work, Franzen has been preoccupied, indeed, sometimes obsessed, with the qualities of his detailing. "Our stairs were invariably designed with 6½ inch risers and 12½ inch treads, because those proportions are the most comfortable and the most graceful", he once explained. The details of his window frames, roof edges, stair rails, and all the rest are just as thoughtfully developed. He had long admired

the sturdy qualities of Romanesque buildings, and tried to transfer that preoccupation to more modern materials and building techniques. The massive supports found in some of Franzen's earlier houses clearly hark back to his admiration for the Romanesque; but that preoccupation soon gave way to a more delicate vocabulary, a vocabulary that had, in fact, shaped his earliest houses, with their minimalist frames of steel.

But not all of Franzen's houses conformed to the Miesian vocabulary of steel and glass by any means. Many of his houses had massive brick walls, floors of stone and wood, plasters ceilings, and variously textured surfaces on partitions and screens. Much of this is reminiscent of the work of Marcel Breuer, the architect who had been one of Franzen's favorite teachers at Harvard and remained one of his friends in the later years. Still, Franzen's houses, unlike those of many of his contemporaries who had studied under Breuer, had a precision of detail that was much closer in spirit to Mies van der Rohe's hard-hedged buildings around Chicago.

And there were other Franzen houses that were reminiscent of the remarkable work of Louis Kahn, the Philadelphia architect who was obsessed with organizing his buildings by the use of vertical ducts and shafts that would serve and support the spaces between them.

Franzen's Dana and Buttenweiser Houses, among others, were dramatically shaped not so much by columns and beams and walls, but by regularly spaced, vertical shafts that contained various mechanical services and storage facilities, and that helped articulate the spaces between them, and incidentally served as supporting structures as well. These articulated structures, a life-long preoccupation of Louis Kahn's, made rather more sense in larger buildings than in houses; and Franzen would employ Kahn's language of articulation more successfully in many of his later works, in laboratory and in manufacturing buildings. But even in some of the earlier residential buildings, Franzen liked to organize his interior spaces by the use of regularly spaced vertical elements, usually containing secondary spaces and utilities, that would give a clear articulation to the houses.

Many of the buildings documented in the next chapter were shaped by systems of vertical service shafts that helped organize and articulate the spaces between them.

Franzen House, Rye, New York 1956

The house is a pavilion on a podium placed in a thickly wooded site with natural rock outcroppings sheltered from its suburban neighbors by small hills.

The sheltering roof is constructed with 2 x 2 x ¼ inch steel angle irons creating a freestanding, three-hinged welded arch system. The freestanding roof supported by eight columns was erected in one day. It permitted work to proceed during inclement weather.

The four bedrooms were enclosed by walls and cabinets to a seven foot height above which glass panels provided enclosure.

The living area, dining space, and seating areas, as well as the kitchen were arranged around freestanding cabinets and a low fireplace wall, thus providing an open plan suitable for entertaining and displaying artworks on freestanding panels.

The intention was to create a structure made of the materials and engineering skills of our time and juxtapose it to the splendid and mature natural setting of the site. Walls and decks reach out into this setting extending the interior spaces. A glass house requires privacy of location. The site here afforded such privacy by being hundreds of feet from the neighborhood road, and by being surrounded by a thick forest of large trees.

16

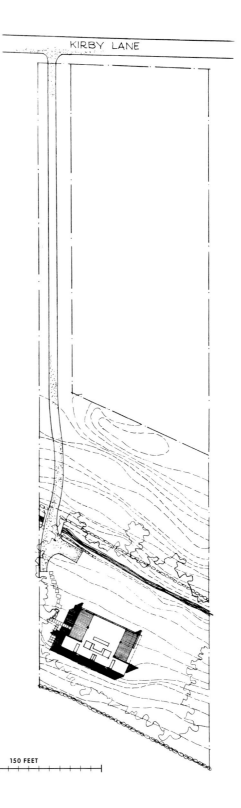

KIRBY LANE

150 FEET

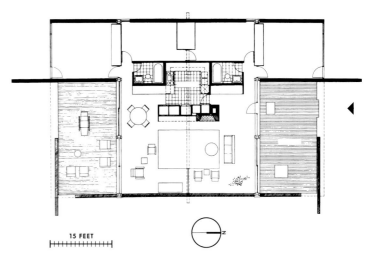

15 FEET

Beattie House, Rye, New York 1958

This house designed for a photographer and his artist wife, as well as several college-age children is set on a sequestered suburban site. Mature trees and the rolling topography presented a perfect site for a pavilion house shielded from neighboring houses.

The central element of this design is a glass-enclosed cube containing the entry, a sunken fireplace seating area, as well as a dining space. This central element is sheltered by a high, floating steel-framed roof supported on four columns. The glass cube is framed by two solid brick boxes containing bedrooms, bath, and kitchen.

The floating roof, the glass cube, and the two brick boxes were intended to have a certain monumental character to set this design apart from the typical suburban kitsch.

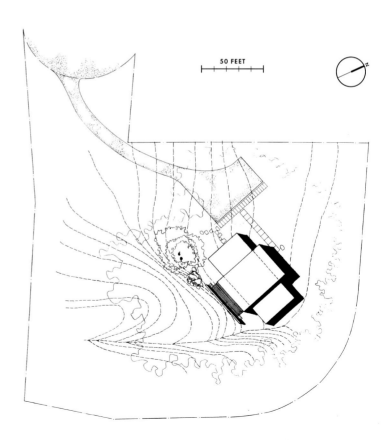

50 FEET

24

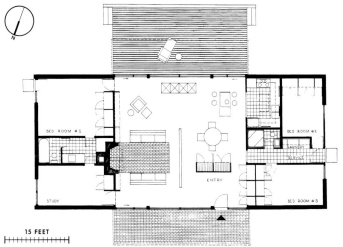

15 FEET

Weissman House, Rye, New York 1959

*The family's extensive space program was a challenge
to the design objective of creating a solution of simplicity
within a tight budget.*

*Therefore the structural system employed is intended as a
unifying element. The steel frame is a continuously welded
system permitting the use of light steel sections throughout.
Exposed and freestanding, it gives the sense of the spread-
out plan of a small house. None of the partitions meet the
high cypress ceiling, and thus the feeling of a family under
one roof is enhanced. The requirements of the program
and client preference dictated a one-story solution on a
rocky ridge in a secluded section of Rye.*

*The design is once again that of a freestanding pavilion
set in nature and sheltering a growing family's life.*

26

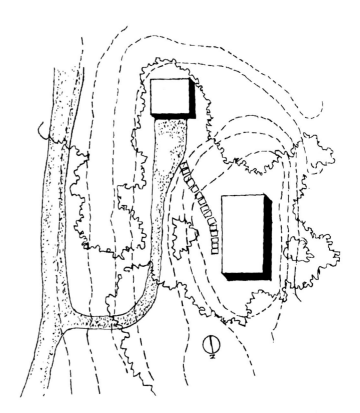

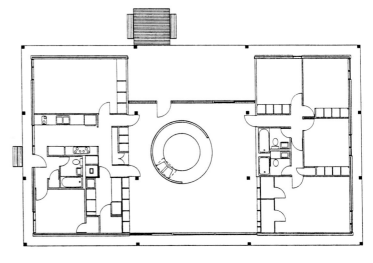

Towers House, Essex, Connecticut 1963

*The site is a mountain top with a magnificent panoramic
vista of the Connecticut River yacht basin, Plum Island,
and Long Island Sound.*

*The layout of the house responds to the demands of the
setting. The active areas such as living room and kitchen
are placed into a glass pavilion on top of the site.*

*The bedroom wing is on the lower level to create a change
of pace. The view from the lower and quieter level is of
closed vistas into the woods and to a pond.*

*The plan is essentially a compact square, surrounded
by a series of retaining walls and terraces,
which extend out into the landscape in pinwheel fashion.*

*The entrance to the house was planned
for a sense of drama: the approach to the building
is from a lower level, away from the water, and the view
is not apparent.*

*From this angle, the forms of the house itself are dominant;
it is not until one goes to the upper level that the marine
view can be seen through deeply shaded glass walls.*

*The structure of the house is a carefully engineered
steel frame, entirely free standing and self-bracing.
It is composed of nine inverted umbrellas
which are linked together as three-hinged arches*

30 *clad in cypress boarding.*

50 FEET

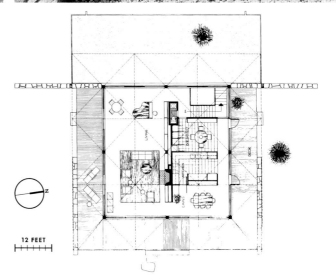

12 FEET

34

Castle House, New London, Connecticut 1964

This house is constructed on a historic rock outcropping
next to an eighteenth century lighthouse facing the open sea.
Much of the small lot was shaped by means of seawalls
and rockfill.
The house is located on a platform so as to remain
several feet above the highest recorded hurricane tides.
The location of the pool, in the open ocean, serves as a buffer
in the worst weather.
Living in such an exposed setting called for a change of pace.
We created intimate views toward carefully underscaled
landscaping along one side of the living room. Furthermore,
since the lot is small, it seemed important to provide a
variety of places in which to be and to sit.
The circular dining porch above the surging tide and rocks
is one such spot.
The freestanding pavilion at the center of the house is
roofed by steel-framed hyperbolic paraboloids clad in
cypress boarding. This central space faces both the ocean
on one side and an intimate walled garden on the other.
The pavilion completes a cycle of houses which were
designed around the notion of a central space with a high
and articulate roof suggesting shelter. The theme
of the varied central space is further developed in later houses
36 *using masonry towers to enclose and define it.*

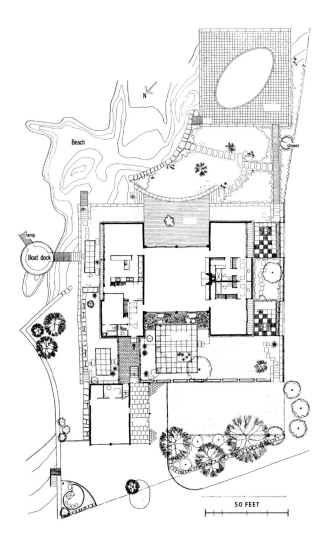

2

Franzen started his independent career designing houses and other relatively small industrial and commercial buildings; and such buildings tend to be primarily shaped by functional and structural concerns. So his earliest buildings were exercises in structural expressions.

But after a few years, his commissions began to include larger buildings, in which the governing discipline was not necessarily structure – but what the architect Louis Kahn used to call "servant spaces", mechanical systems, in particular, which required repetitive assemblies of shafts for air-exhaust and air-intake, for heating and cooling, and for separating and supporting various other services like elevators, cables, fire stairs, and all the rest. In those buildings, the mechanical systems (or servant spaces) would be pulled out of the basic plan (the served space), and both would be separately articulated. "Kahn's work appealed to me because he was another theologian of visual form," Franzen has said, "he was much like the painter Mark Rothko in that respect."

Under the influence of Kahn's work, Franzen began to develop buildings in which the repetitive "served" and "servant" spaces became the most visible elements of the architecture. Kahn had brilliantly pioneered this new language of service shafts, but his pioneering examples had not always functioned especially well: the clusters of vertical services in some of Kahn's laboratory buildings at the University of Pennsylvania, for example, tended to crowd the usable laboratory spaces between them, and rob the laboratory floors of the kind of openness and flexibility that the scientists who were working there needed most.

In his Agronomy Building, for the State College at Cornell, Franzen attempted to expand Kahn's system of vertical services and make the spaces served considerably more open and flexible. And not only that: he also found ways of "expressing" the vertical service shafts in ways that seem more sculptural, more powerful, in fact more beautiful than the towers that Kahn had built at the University of Pennsylvania, which clearly influenced Franzen. The Agronomy Building became a sort of brick pipe organ, with the brick "pipes" grouped together in powerful, sculptural clusters.

Although Franzen explained those brick clusters in functional terms, the fact is that he had always been fascinated by the work of contemporary sculptors and painters, many of them his close friends. Their work influenced his architecture from the very start, and continues to do so. Unquestionably, the huge brick assemblages at Cornell were shaped as much by Franzen's sculptural interests as they were by purely technical requirements.

And they were shaped by another concern as well: the Cornell State College campus had always been considered a rather minor adjunct to the high-class university next door. By making his brick pipe organ a highly visible element on the Ithaca skyline, Franzen in effect gave the State College a presence it had lacked until then. It has been difficult to ignore the State College ever since its towers were built.

Franzen's buildings at Cornell, among the best structures done in the U.S. in the second half of the century, are remarkable not only because they are sculpturally impressive (which they unquestionably are); but also because they successfully solve extremely complex technical problems, so difficult to solve in themselves, that have often escaped solutions by some better known architects.

Franzen was quite aware of the technical problems involved in the Agronomy Tower (now called "Bradfield Hall"). He said that "people assumed that all laboratory facilities should be more or less alike. Actually the exact opposite is true. The specific mission of these labs at Cornell was to serve research in biology, chemistry, biochemistry, plant breeding, and genetics. So the labs had to accommodate a great variety of equipment and of lab arrangements." Experiments in biology and biochemistry are conducted over long periods of time, and require very precise climate control, as well as immunity from all contamination. They have to be sealed against such contamination, and they require windowless, air-conditioned spaces. On the other hand, they also call for office spaces for the technicians working there. In short, they need to serve separate but related needs, each with its own climate and climate control. Multi-discipline labs, like those in the Agronomy Tower, have to offer the utmost in flexibility.

The labs in the Agronomy Tower do offer such flexibility. Basically, they are located on a stack of loft spaces that are air-conditioned from a central spine, and further served by externally applied brick ducts containing pipes, wires, and smaller ducts. There is a double-loaded corridor that runs north-south down the center of each floor; and at each end of the corridor there is a vertical shaft that supplies cold and warm air.

There are the laboratory services, on the east and west sides of the Agronomy Tower, and contained in vertical, brick-clad "risers" that are applied to the sides of the tower. Finally, there is a deep "cavity wall" that runs north-south along the outer edges of the loft spaces. It provides access to all the laboratory services that rise up in the applied ducts and serve all the laboratories contained in the loft spaces.

45

This sounds complicated, but it is, in fact, a very clear, simply organized, and highly efficient part of a 13-story tall brick "machine" that is innovative both in terms of its structure and its services. In most cases where complex laboratories have been built, the result has been either a dull, curtainwall-enclosed "package" of little scale or any other quality, or a jumble of pipes and ducts and cables that add up to nothing more than enclosed chaos. The Agronomy Tower instead, is a powerful, beautiful, and supremely well-organized work of architecture and industrial design.

Because most of the ducts, pipes, and cables were applied to all four sides of the laboratory block, there was no particular reason to treat the sides differently from each other. And so, in this building, the facades are basically assemblages of brick shafts and panels, with only glass walls at the ends of the central spine of corridors, to provide light for the faculty lounges located there.

In another one of Franzen's buildings at Cornell, the building known as the Multi-categorical Research Laboratory at Cornell's College of Veterinary Medicine, the block is divided down its center by an access corridor, with a variety of laboratories along one side, and offices on the other. This "multi-categorical" building was completed in 1973, half a dozen years after the Agronomy Building was finished.

One side of the building, which was called "Multi-Cat" in an issue of *Architecture PLUS* magazine, is treated much in the way in which Franzen treated the facades of the Agronomy Tower: solid brick walls, accentuated by air-intakes and protrusions of horizontal and vertical supply ducts behind the brick. This side of the building contains sealed laboratories. But the other side of Multi-Cat, which contains offices and similar facilities and faces north, is clad in gray-tinted glass, pretty much in the way office blocks have been clad all over the world, only more elegantly. Three tall "snorkels" stand outside the nine-story glass wall. They are air intakes and are painted a bright vermillion. They are, of course, pieces of minimalist sculpture.

In retrospect, it may not seem all that unusual to treat two sides of the same building in such a different manner. Le Corbusier had frequently done so. The Pavilion Suisse, in Paris, is basically a slab building whose two opposite sides are treated quite differently. But in a time dominated by Miesian "universal" design, Franzen's completely different detailing of the opposing sides of Multi-Cat seemed quite surprising. It suggested a degree of flexibility that had been largely lacking during the years when the "packaging" of buildings was the norm, and orientation only rarely

influenced the shapes and details of facades. But in the buildings done for Cornell, and in several other buildings completed in the 1970s and 1980s, Franzen responded to a number of concerns that were not especially influential among his contemporaries: contextual concerns, environmental concerns, and what might be called "collage concerns" – or a fascination with "collage" as a new way of looking at a world shaped as much by differences in all things, as by similarities.

Franzen was designing and building his architectural "collages" while many of his contemporaries were designing and building what they called "postmodernist" structures, which tended to be assemblages of deliberately inconsistent architectural "happenings" – structures lacking unity or visible coherence. (In fact, of course, the architectural "happenings" of postmodernists were very carefully assembled to look incoherent!) Franzen was quite as aware as the postmodernists that there were often inherent programmatic contradictions in buildings; but he felt that the difficult job of an architect, in such conflicting situations, was to create a very special coherence. And his "collage buildings" were a deliberate attempt to create that kind of unity, to arrive at Aalto's "simultaneous solution of opposites."

These "collage buildings" made perfectly good sense, of course: there is really no reason why the different sides of a building (that clearly face in different directions) must necessarily be similar. In fact, it would seem more important for the different sides of a given building to relate, visually, to the sides of different neighboring buildings that help shape the same adjacent space.

In Franzen's laboratory buildings, the necessarily elaborate mechanical and electrical systems usually shaped one side of the structure. But there were other considerations as well. Multi-Cat and the Agronomy Building are located at opposite ends of Tower Road, which forms an axis on the

Cornell campus. The approaches to Multi-Cat are largely determined by urbanistic considerations relating to the campus plan – if and when that plan is finalized, which may not be for some time.

What makes Franzen's "collage buildings" so interesting is that most of them seem to resolve inherent contradictions that defeated many other architects. In the second half of the twentieth century, if you were a Mies disciple, your buildings had to be uncompromisingly Miesian, regardless of the function, context, or site. They were monuments to unity, or perhaps to uniformity.

But Franzen's "collage buildings" were not simple-minded at all. They confronted complexity and contradiction and resolved seemingly insoluble problems surprisingly, creatively, and convincingly. His buildings are not awkward compromises or accidents, but convincing works of art, however multi-faceted they may appear at first glance. The ultimate coherence came out of Franzen's ability to resolve complexities and contradictions, and was due, more importantly, to his insistence upon a perfection of detail in every aspect of his structures. That perfection of detail is a unifying force that can also be found in the best Miesian buildings, but very rarely in the work of postmodernists. Franzen's buildings do not celebrate "complexity" and "contradiction", they seem to celebrate "complexity" and resolution, more difficult to achieve than "contradiction."

"Even the programmatic aspects of single buildings is one of opposites and contradictions", Franzen has said. "This really reflects the human condition today. I have found myself excited by the possibilities of combining different formal systems into a single compositional framework. By going into the texture and the meaning of a broader canvas, I have found that architectural compositions are enriched by acknowledging the antagonism between form and purpose and ambiguities of reality, and the need for both history and future." The "ambiguities of reality,"

a rather more sophisticated definition of the essence of architecture today. More sophisticated than earlier rules that defined form solely by function.

Helen Whiting Dress Factory
Pleasantville, New York 1963

The interior and exterior walls of this plant are unpainted concrete block bearing walls. Most of the building is an open loft framed by the modular wall system and deep, glued, laminated beams. Glass panels are set between alternate beams and provide natural light for the workers. This building represents an effort to achieve an architectural expression using very low-cost materials and finishes in a building type that is often neglected.

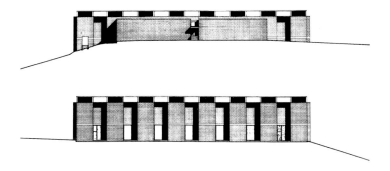

49

Bernstein House, Great Neck, New York 1963

The site of this house lies in a fully developed area on Long Island with an architectural character suggesting "Golf-Course Colonial".
It seemed crucial to affirm a more basic approach.
The house itself is for a large family, and the site is the crest of a hill looking toward New York City.
The essential design is that of a wall through which you enter from the street to find the grand vistas. The living spaces are on the entrance level facing the view, while the children's areas are on the lower level.
Eight square modular units organize the plan and are further expressed on the exterior. The result is a cohesive, but rhythmic design with vaulted wood ceilings resting on concrete block bearing walls.

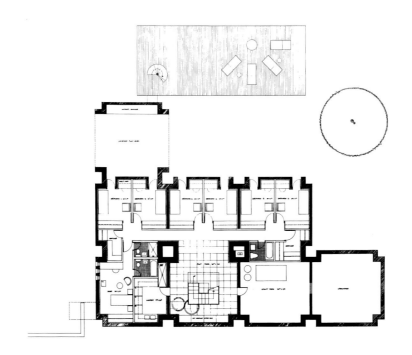

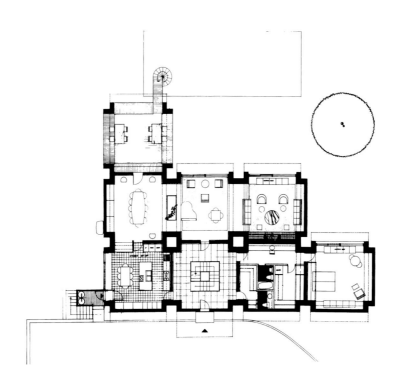

Dana House, New Canaan, Connecticut 1963

This house is situated on an old and flat farmland in the midst of an apple orchard. Private rooms and service spaces in five modular masonry towers are arranged around the central living area and form a pavilion for general family activities. The landscape is taken into consideration in the disposition of volumes, with varied glimpses of vistas over the fields or through the orchards.

This house, as well as the Buttenweiser House, was a step in the development of the pavilion house. In this case the central space is contained by the towers arranged in an asymmetrical pattern designed to quicken and animate the heart of the scheme.

54

12 FEET

Buttenweiser House
Mamaroneck, New York 1965

The site is a rocky island approached on a causeway. The island is covered by high tides every year, and the site is subject to frequent battering by waves during storms. The design therefore raises the living areas a full story above the rocks and permits high tides to pass underneath the living-dining element. The raised levels of the house permitted siting of the various elements in such a way as to open views across Long Island Sound.

The house is for a large family; the program has been articulated into towers representing family bedrooms, guest and study areas, as well as a service element containing kitchen, laundry, and maid's quarters.

The living areas, including sundecks, are centrally located between the towers providing access to each.

Construction is of reinforced concrete in order to withstand the occasionally heavy sea action. The towers are clad in brick, whereas the living room and dining room element is of exposed architectural concrete.

58

61

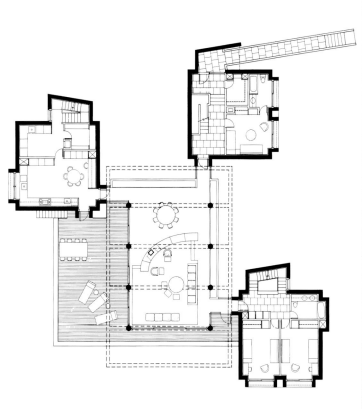

Agronomy Building, State College
Cornell University, Ithaca, New York 1968

The Agronomy Building complex (now called Bradfield Hall) contains three major elements: the two lower elements are the administrative wing and form an entrance portico. Another low element, which relates in height to the adjoining agricultural campus buildings, contains both teaching and administrative functions. These low elements are clipped onto the pedestrian routes established by campus plan, facilitating easy access on foot to all levels.

The third element is the high graduate research tower. The intended image of the tower is to proclaim the vitality of the State College campus while establishing a focal point that relates it to the neighboring campus of Cornell University.

The Agronomy Building is an action structure, a building that does not just sit there, but seems to be doing something. This effect is simply brought about by arranging functional components into expressive forms.

The tower's mechanical systems become an intricate part of the design, a distinctive feature on all sides of the exterior. The 13-story tower contains laboratories for research in soil-related biology. The nature of the research required windowless laboratories.

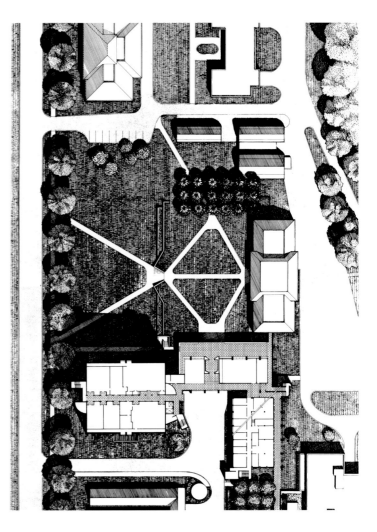

67

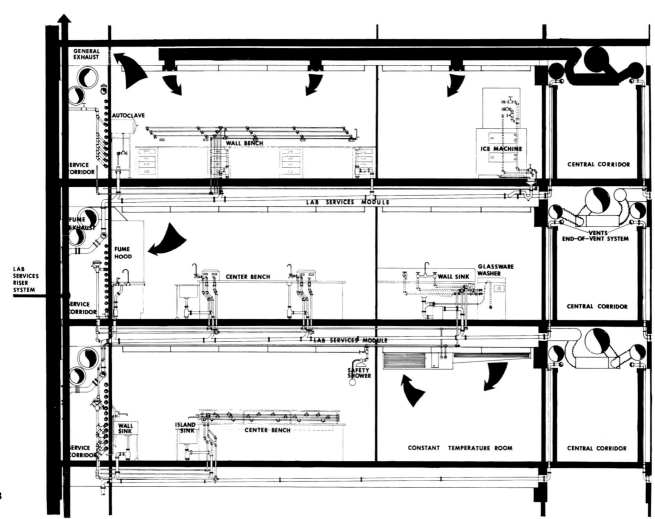

GENERAL EXHAUST

AUTOCLAVE

WALL BENCH

ICE MACHINE

SERVICE CORRIDOR

CENTRAL CORRIDOR

LAB SERVICES MODULE

FUME EXHAUST

FUME HOOD

CENTER BENCH

WALL SINK

GLASSWARE WASHER

VENTS
END-OF-VENT SYSTEM

LAB SERVICES RISER SYSTEM

SERVICE CORRIDOR

CENTRAL CORRIDOR

LAB SERVICES MODULE

SAFETY SHOWER

WALL SINK

ISLAND SINK

CENTER-BENCH

CONSTANT TEMPERATURE ROOM

CENTRAL CORRIDOR

SERVICE CORRIDOR

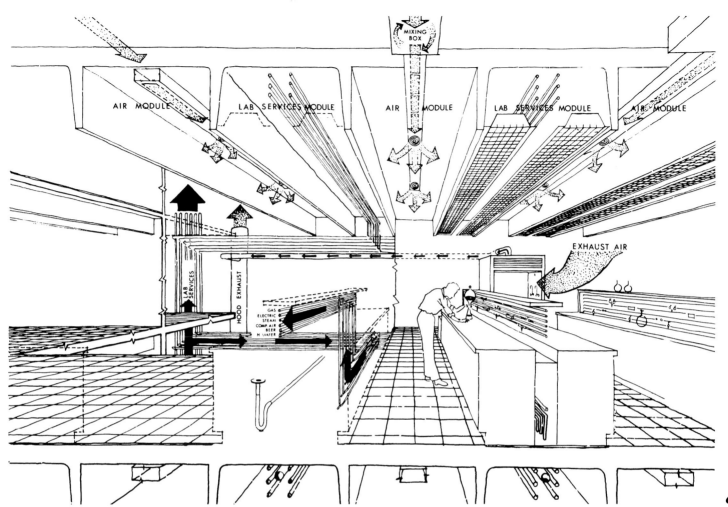

AIR MODULE LAB SERVICES MODULE AIR MODULE LAB SERVICES MODULE AIR MODULE

MIXING BOX

LAB SERVICES

HOOD EXHAUST

GAS
ELECTRIC
STEAM
COMP. AIR
BEER
H. WATER

EXHAUST AIR

69

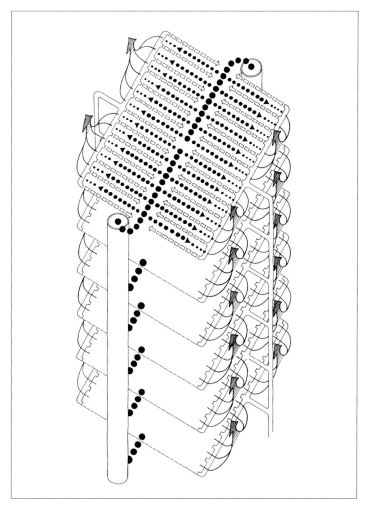

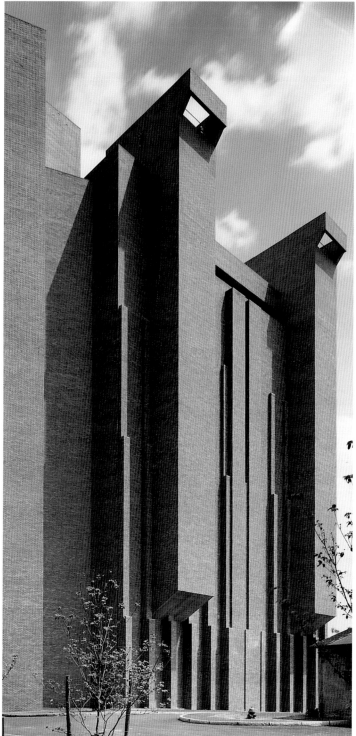

71

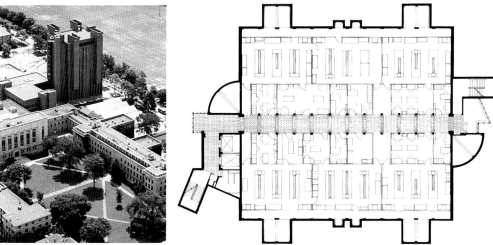

First Unitarian Church of Richmond
Richmond, Virginia 1970

This church was meant to be not just for a weekend congregation, but a daily meeting place. Therefore spaces have been designed for multiple uses such as art studios, adult education, as well as religious instruction. The main church hall has a fixed seating of 250, and additional flexible seating for 60, and can be used as an auditorium, concert hall, or setting for a wedding.
The character of the complex is rambling and low – appropriate with economic construction as well as the character of the community. The church was built of concrete block, left exposed on the interior. It is hoped that the focal point of this center will not be a church steeple, but the activity and life it generates.

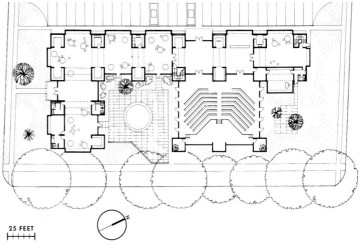

25 FEET

75

Harpers Ferry Center
Harpers Ferry, West Virginia 1969 – 1972

*The Harpers Ferry Center was conceived as a key element
in the National Parks Service's effort to integrate its
various interpretive services into the Park System.
The building brings together a great variety of professionals
– historians, graphic artists, and film makers – in a studio
setting.*

*The spectacular site on the brow of the hills above Harpers
Ferry overlooks the Shenandoah River. The undulating form
of the crest of the hills determined the disposition of facade
elements. In addition, the building relates to an axial system
of roads and historic buildings laid out at the end of the
eighteenth century. Thus the entrance side of the building
receives and accepts a rectilinear system. The structure then
acknowledges the organic topography while at the same time
engaging the larger field of a man-made grid iron plan.*

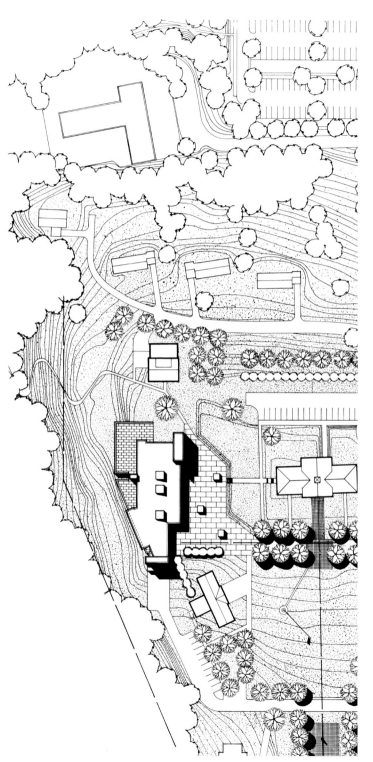

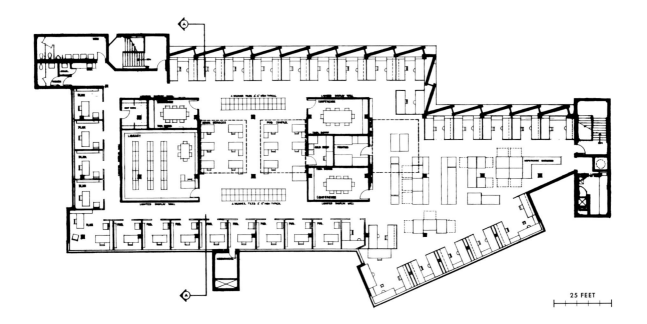

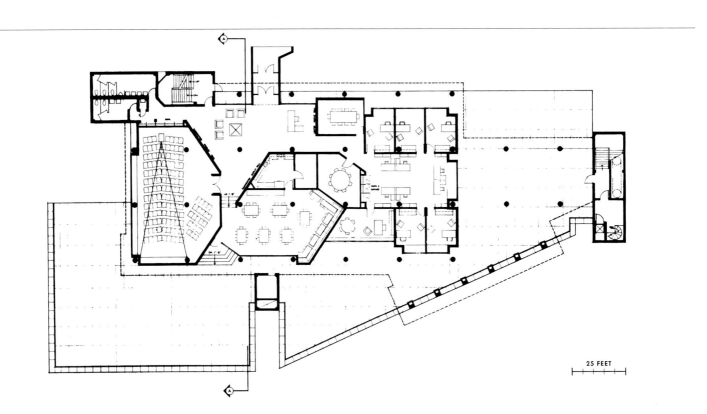

University of New Hampshire, Residence Halls and Dining Hall, Durham, N. H. 1969 – 1972

This is a low-budget, co-educational dormitory for approximately 450 students at this state university. The project is part of a larger plan prepared by the architect for a new residential quadrangle. The basic planning module began with the design of a required two-people room. The two-people room was designed as two nooks where each student would have his or her own identifiable corner or turf.

The grouping of students per floor was reduced to 24, with their own laundry, kitchenette, and small living area.

In order to permit the floors to represent the smaller groups, the common facilities were designed as a sequence of intimate and small spaces.

The design is organized by the shape of the land.

This dormitory and the additional ones straddle a change in level, and surround a natural clearing which in turn became the central pedestrian quadrangle from the vehicular access at the lower level of the site.

At the center of the pedestrian quadrangle lies the new dining hall. This dining hall is arranged so that the students can eat and socialize in a series of small spaces and even nooks adjoining the cafeteria. While the entire residential quadrangle is very large, every effort has been made to retain a small, friendly scale.

84

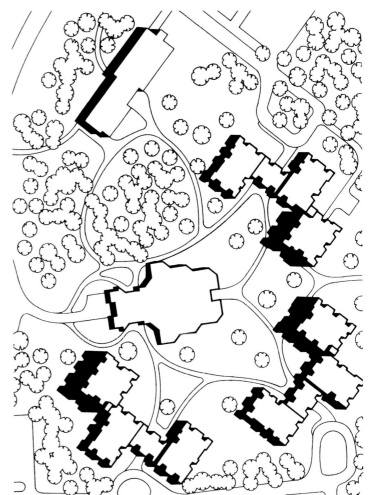

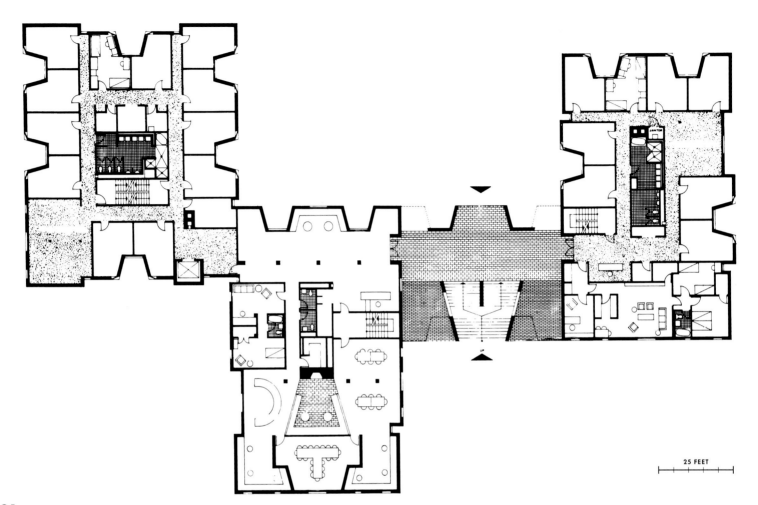

25 FEET

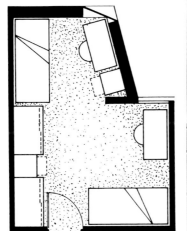

91

During the first half of this century, it was routine for modern architects to be involved in several related arts and disciplines as well: architects (like Le Corbusier, Aalto, Gropius, and others) were important industrial designers as well as designers of buildings. Architects like Behrens, Breuer, Max Bill, and Le Corbusier (again) did some of their most interesting work in painting, sculpture, graphic design, and other two- or three-dimensional arts. And some, like Antoni Gaudí, worked in a great many different disciplines that were almost indistinguishable from each other.

But many of these interdisciplinary pursuits seemed to become less interesting to most architects in the second half of the century. And this lack began to show in the quality of the buildings they designed. In fact, some architects, especially among postmodernists, appeared quite ignorant of related arts and disciplines. Except for a few exceptions like Eero Saarinen and Charles Eames, modern architects of the second or third generation were almost embarrassingly illiterate when it came to the other arts.

For several reasons, Ulrich Franzen, who had started out as a student of art history at Williams College before he began his studies in architecture at Harvard, continued to be significantly involved with the other visual arts in much of his work. Not as a painter or as a graphic designer, but as an active patron of painting, sculpture, and even, on occasion, as a patron of industrial design as well. As early as the 1960s, he arranged for the Architectural League, in New York, where he served as president, to mount an exhibition of Christo's work, which was then barely known even among the most sophisticated museum curators in Manhattan. In later years, Franzen began to incorporate work by minimalist painters and sculptors in his buildings, and persuaded the Whitney Museum of American Art, as mentioned earlier, to establish a network of branch museums both in New York and outside the city, and to incorporate these branches in commercial buildings designed for those locations. In fact, in much of his work as an architect, he included the work of some of the radical artists of the day, many of whom did not become very widely known until much later – and some of whom are hardly known to the art world to this day. While some other architects of Franzen's generation, like his former Harvard schoolmates Philip Johnson and his Harvard teacher, I. M. Pei, would often include the work of important contemporary painters and sculptors like Pablo Picasso or Henry Moore in their architecture, Franzen went out of his way to engage laser artists like Bob Whitman and pop artists like Les Levine, hardly known at the time, to enliven his buildings.

Franzen involved some of the avant-garde artists of his day in a great many of his projects from the 1950s on. As a result, he became friends with them and with museum and gallery people in New York. Among them were Arne and Millie Glimcher, who opened the Pace Gallery in the early 1960s. It soon became one of the most avant-garde galleries in Manhattan, showing totally new, experimental work. One of the Pace artists was Bob Whitman, who showed work with lasers that marked tracks on the gallery walls. That is where Franzen first encountered such experimental work.

During those same years, the U.S. Information Agency invited about a dozen architects and artists (including Whitman) to submit proposals for the design of the official U.S. Pavilion to be built at the Osaka World Fair in Japan in 1970. While other competitors proposed a fairly predictable range of contemporary structures, domes, tents, tetrahedra, etc., Franzen and Whitman designed an "electronic experience" involving laser beams that would draw lines on the inner surfaces of a half-buried bubble, while the sound of torrents of water would come gushing out from some inner or outer sanctum. All of this baffled the assembled competition jurors, who proceeded to select a more conventional design to represent the United States of America: an inflatable tent that made no gushing noises.

When finally built, or inflated, budgetary considerations forced the U.S. Information Agency to reduce the original tent or bubble to a rather flat blister, which apparently made more sense to the jurors than the Franzen-Whitman "electronic experience."

In 1970 Franzen designed a clothing store for Paraphernalia, a company that was known for extremely avant-garde designs and products. He called the store an "experiment in electrographic architecture," which suggested, quite rightly, that the Paraphernalia installation employed all kinds of electric and electronic devices and gadgets and images that had rarely seen the light of day (or of night) outside the most outrageous New York nightclubs, like the Electric Circus – an installation which Franzen and his pals visited regularly, with open eyes (and ears).

While all this was going on, Franzen designed a house for the Glimchers (which was not built), and then another house on Long Island which was. That house (and several other buildings designed by Franzen over the years) is remarkable not only for the paintings and sculpture that enrich the building, but also for its rather surprising bilateral symmetry. In those years, modern architects, by and large, were not supposed to be doing symmetrical buildings; but Franzen, who may have violated more rules of thumb than just about anyone else of his generation, did not seem to be bothered by departures from accepted norms.

Although the Glimcher House is not a gallery, it contains several impressive works of art, and the grounds were treated as a sculpture park, with a kind of walk-in environment created by Jean Dubuffet, as well as works by Louise Nevelson, Joan Miró, Jim Dine, and others. It is not the only building of those years in which Franzen was able to include the work of various artists to enhance the architecture. In the First City National Bank in Binghamton, New York, he commissioned the weaver Helena Hernmarck to make a 90 foot long, photo-realist tapestry that is, in effect, a panoramic view from the Bank across the Chenango River, or rather, as that view might appear if the Bank had not been built to block it. In the University Center, at the University of Michigan in Flint, the semi-circular courtyard that faces southwest was to have contained a chrome-plated sculpture of an early Buick, which would have been a wonderfully appropriate image if it had, in fact, been installed. Alas, it wasn't: the clients felt that a chrome-plated pop sculpture might have looked like a joke (and, hence, apparently inappropriate, in a General Motors emporium where automobile production is taken very seriously). And in various buildings designed by Franzen for Philip Morris and for several university campuses, works of art were usually installed or proposed to establish scale or identity or points of reference. At Hunter College, Franzen asked the artist Barbara Stauffacher to design all the graphics for the new buildings. Stauffacher had invented what became known as "Super Graphics," and her work at Hunter College was done in "graffiti style."

Although Franzen's early buildings tended to be Euclidean and often Miesian in their angular geometry, he became increasingly fascinated by organic, sculptural forms in the 1960s, forms far removed from the rectilinear discipline associated with Mies van der Rohe's work. Franzen was not the only one whose architecture became more and more sculptural: starting in the 1950s, Le Corbusier began to design and build increasingly plastic buildings, in India, and in Europe as well. And Wright had done a number of "free-form" buildings in the final years of his career that stood in dramatic contrast to the urban grid-geometry in which they stood – the Guggenheim Museum, in Manhattan, being the best known of these "free-form" buildings, but by no means the only one.

The most amazing piece of sculptural architecture done by Franzen in that phase of his career is, without doubt, the

Alley Theatre in Houston, Texas, designed in 1965. At first glance it seems not unlike the Guggenheim, a building that has often been compared to a concrete snail. But upon closer inspection, the Alley Theatre turns out to be quite symmetrical in plan and almost Euclidean in many of its details; still, it is clearly thought of as a work of "free form" sculpture in an urban space that would soon be shaped by tall office slabs and similar, predictable downtown towers. And that, of course, is precisely what happened. The Theatre is an impressive piece of concrete sculpture, in dramatic contrast to the typical office slabs that have sprung up all around it.

Franzen designed and built several other "free-form" structures in the 1960s: the Bloedel Guest House, in Williamstown, Massachusetts, is one of these, Franzen's entry to the FDR Memorial competition, which was to have been built on the Potomac, in Washington, D. C., is another; and there were other projects that were major departures from his earlier, geometric buildings. Obviously, he felt free to experiment with numerous sculptural forms that were and are surprisingly different from his earlier configurations. Concrete technology opened up a broader range of forms than had been determined by steel framing. But none of his later buildings were as sculpturally free as the Alley Theatre in Houston.

Admittedly, the concrete exterior surfaces of the Theatre were not as well finished as they might have been, a flaw found also in much of Le Corbusier's work in Chandigarh. Still, the Alley Theatre is an accomplished work of sculpture, as accomplished as anything of the sort shaped in those years – and containing spaces that easily match those found in many of the free-form buildings of the same period. But, above all, it is an extremely self-assured building, much more self-assured than anything you would expect to find in the work of someone who had never touched a free-form concrete building of that scale in his career before.

Bloedel Guest House
Williamstown, Massachusetts 1965

The design of this three-bedroom guest cottage starts with a high, central element containing a skylit fireplace area and hearth. Curved shapes spin out from this point, and they contain the various rooms all of which are finished with vertical cedar planking and open toward a variety of views. The plan of the house is organic and non-rectilinear, creating interior spaces that are not static but continuous. The full and rounded shapes recall the sculptural shingle architecture of the nineteenth century.

Although this architecture is strongly related to its setting, it is also intended to be an assertive sculptural form, distinctly man-made to contrast with a breathtaking setting.

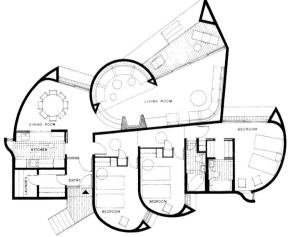

10 FEET

101

Alley Theatre, Houston, Texas 1968

The Alley Theatre is composed of an 800-seat auditorium with an open stage and a 300-seat arena. The two theatres share backstage facilities and are separated by a covered driveway that allows the ticket office to be accessible by car. Designed to be part of the Citys Civic Center, the building's thick walls and deeply shaded openings serve to combat Houston's extreme heat and sunlight. Nine towers, containing stairs and mechanical riser, act as abutments for the long roof spans.

The large 800-seat room was designed to extend the Alley's experience with theatre-in-the-round productions to an additional dimension. The large room is an open stage, with calipers surrounding the audience.

The building design rejects a "Lincoln Center look" and attempts to engage the American Southwest and its neighboring Mexico.

The theatre's urban setting was a major design concern. The Alley is connected by a tunnel to the large parking garage underneath the Civic Center open space. The design acknowledges in height and scale its immediate Civic Center neighbors, namely the Jones Hall for the Performing Arts, a music and concert hall, as well as the Convention Center. These adjoining structures are travertine-clad while the

Alley Theatre is of a light colored cast-in-place concrete.

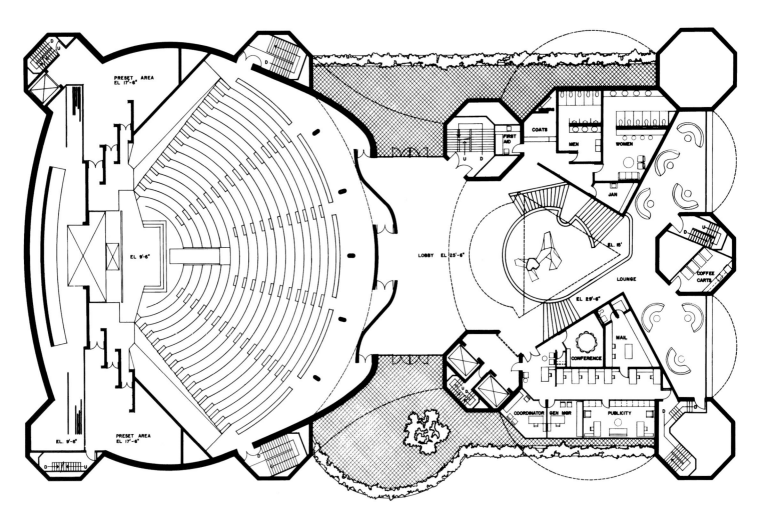

PRESET AREA
EL 17'-6"

EL 9'-6"

PRESET AREA
EL 17'-6"

EL. 9'-6"

FIRST AID

COATS

MEN

WOMEN

JAN

LOBBY EL 125'-6"

EL. 15'

LOUNGE

COFFEE CARTS

EL. 20'-6"

CONFERENCE

MAIL

COORDINATOR

GEN MGR

PUBLICITY

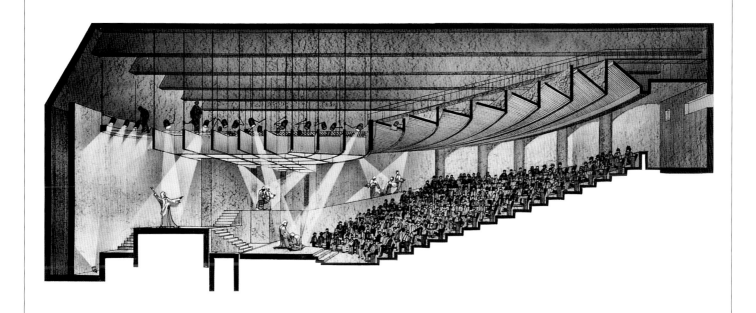

107

Paraphernalia
New York, New York   1968 – 1970

*Paraphernalia stores were boutiques featuring very
avant-garde fashions – many brought over from England.
Among the young designers were Mary Quant
and Betsy Johnson. The shop was an experiment in
"electrographic architecture."
The basic notion was to create a magic box on the sidewalk
with moving images illustrating the clothing for sale. Upon
entering the store, each customer was handed a remote
control for the various projections to enable her to run
through the entire line of products in the hope that this
would be of enough interest and stimulus to then lead her to
the racks of clothing contained in the stainless-steel half
cylinders. Fortunately, the store at street level was
surrounded by tall buildings, so that direct sunlight did not
interfere with the images projected.
In addition to designing the store itself, the architect
designed the symbol and logo for Paraphernalia as well as
the store fittings and the furniture.*

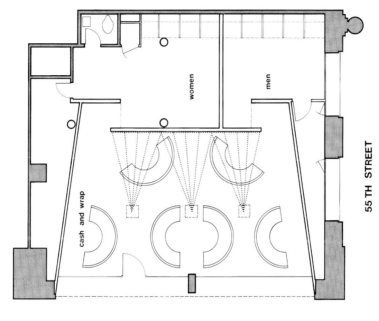

women

men

cash and wrap

55 TH STREET

LEXINGTON AVENUE

111

Franzen Penthouse
New York, New York 1974 – 1975

This apartment was conceived as a spacious oasis away from the hustle and bustle of the city.

The major space of approximately 50 × 35 foot is a fluid open plan. Within this open plan configuration, separate elements like the dining room, the library and TV room, as well as a formal living area were placed. The space extends visually onto the terraces to the north by means of a new glass wall.

Since this is an architect's apartment, certain elements while being decorative or spatial in purpose have other meanings as well.

For instance, the round column enclosed in mirror-finished stainless steel is there to honor Mies van der Rohe.

112

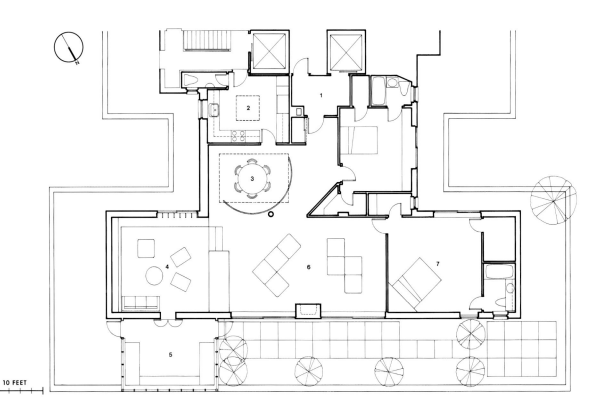

10 FEET

First City National Bank of Binghamton
Binghamton, New York 1974

*This headquarters building was placed in an urban renewal
area. The area and the site included the river bank of the
Chenango River, and there was a requirement to reclaim
this stretch as a community amenity.*
*The bank was designed as a structure that, on the riverside,
acknowledges the reclaimed river and its shore by creating
a public promenade, as well as a terrace for the bank and
its employees. The riverside facade is furthermore made up
of floors stepped back to create a gentle relationship
between building and river. On the other hand the cityside
is designed to be an active and lively complement to
downtown, with the banking room as focal point.*

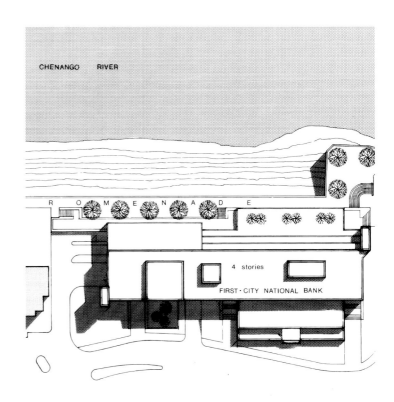

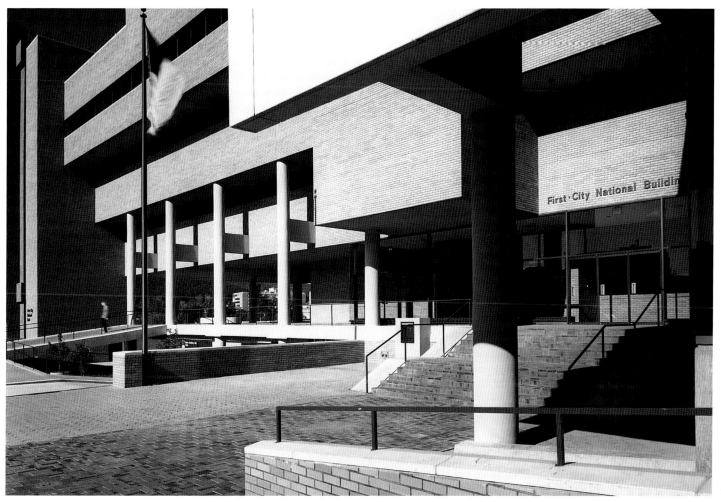

115

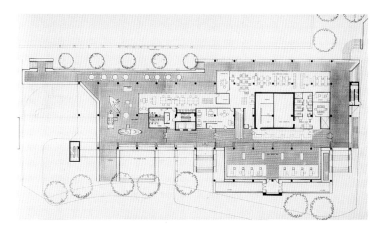

Multi-categorical Research Tower, Cornell University, Ithaca, New York 1974–1975

This building for the College of Veterinary Medicine at Cornell University contains completely controlled and sealed laboratory environments for virus research on the one hand, and offices for professors and graduate students on the other.

Programmatically these two elements constitute opposites of use and function. The design fully acknowledges the diverse programmatic elements by arranging two entirely different building types and their facades along a central corridor spine.

The grey tinted glass facade of the office element faces north and overlooks a lake that contrasts sharply with the southern facade. The south facade is in part organized by a complex air ventilation system including highly specialized exhaust systems, culminating in a cornice-like exhaust element at the top of the south wall.

The nature of the research required sealed laboratories with 100 percent fresh air – all of which had to be taken in and expelled from the top of the structure.

The research tower is situated at the end of Tower Road, the main east-west axis of the Cornell campus, uniting the endowed and the state campuses. The north facade of the building is inflected to terminate the vista along this axis.

118

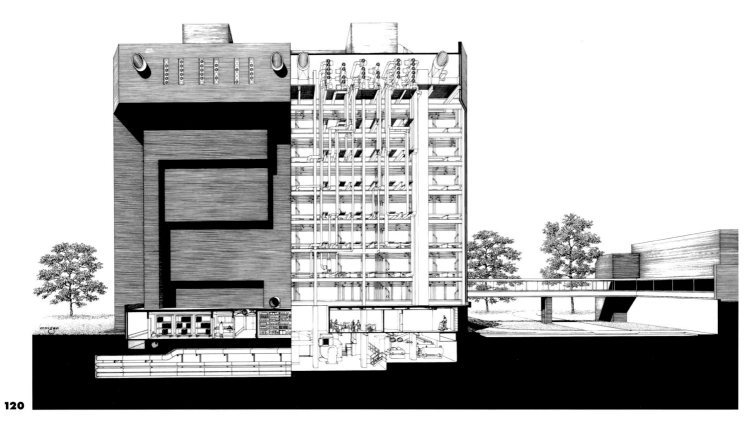

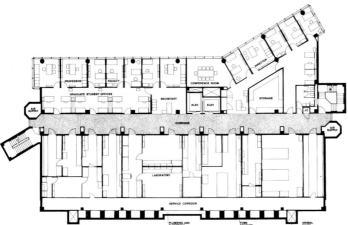

121

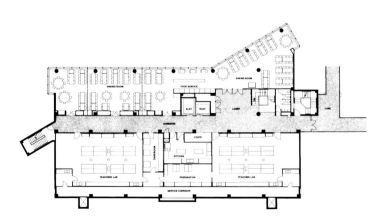

Harlem School of the Arts
New York, New York 1974 – 1978

This school provides a unique arts program for the children in its community. The building was designed to maintain the character of its block frontage and not to overwhelm the modest neighboring buildings. Classrooms and offices look inward to an atrium garden with an architect-designed waterfall hugging a rugged escarpment of rock that rises 45 feet high and forms the rear property line. The lobby is a naturally lit two-story high space which also acts as a gathering place for various school activities and performances.

The architectural concept was to create a safe and inviting oasis away from the overwhelming scale of the surrounding city. The street wall of the building is impenetrable except for the entry, so as to enhance the experience of entering the lobby space and then discovering the cloistered garden and its waterfall.

The school provides three dance studios of various sizes, the largest also being a multi-purpose space 20 feet high, serving the chorus, orchestra, and dramatics. The shape and acoustics of the space are altered by means of sliding walls. On the ground floor is the space for the visual art program, adult art program, and art exibition area. The second floor is devoted almost entirely to music. There are sound-isolated practice rooms, as well as a music recital space.

124

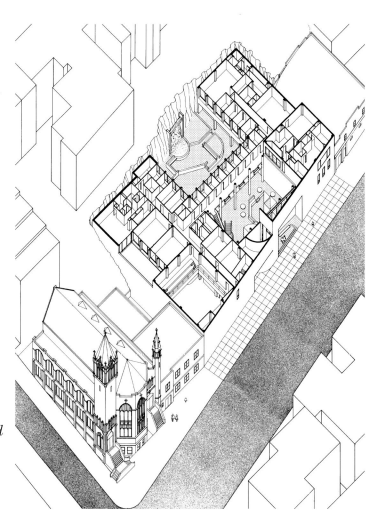

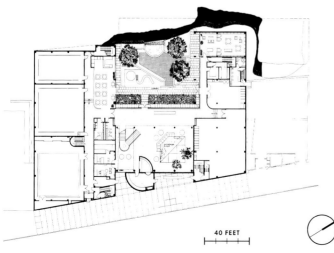

40 FEET

Franzen House, Bridgehampton, Long Island, New York 1978 — 1979

This house is located on the bay side of a narrow barrier beach that is subject to occasional flooding.

The conceptual idea of the house is that of a structure "floating" on a sea of low and dense vegetation in an area of great sweeping horizontality. The views toward the bay and the ocean encompass more water than land, enhancing the feeling of being aboard a ship.

While the house is winterized, it is intended as a modest-sized summer and weekend place. Four different decks for viewing and sun-bathing are offering appropriate settings and shelters for the varying climate. The house is in effect a 40 × 60 foot rectangle of which the fully enclosed area is some 1,800 square feet. It is constructed on wolmanized wooden piles, with a heavy girder platform on which the wood-framed house is set. The exterior material is vertical cedar siding, stained white. The interior surfaces are generally painted sheetrock, with the exception of the major spaces where ceilings and pylons are clad with painted wood boarding. The focal point of the entry deck is a circular cutout to frame the bay view for a first glimpse. The house itself is a wall facing the street with panoramic views suddenly apparent through large glass walls when you step inside.

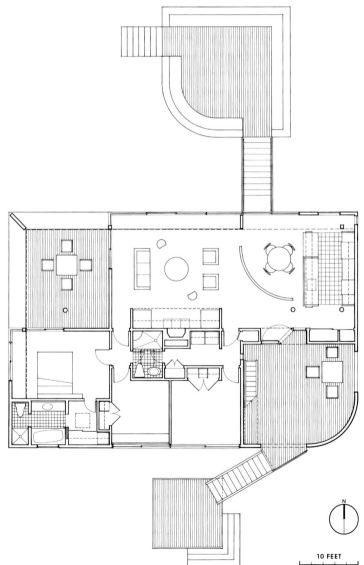

10 FEET

Krauss House, Old Westbury, New York 1978

This residence is located where a 47-room, nineteenth century mansion once stood. The house incorporates two remaining rooms from the old mansion which were saved from demolition and purchased together with the land. The house generally occupies the footprint of the old mansion and recaptures its views. The overall composition of the house is an attempt to incorporate discreet remnants of another era with new structures, into an integrated assembly of parts.

The two rooms of the old mansion were substantially restored and organized into a study and a parlor-living room. The program for the new spaces, attached to the old by a link, contains bedrooms for three children, maid quarters, a second floor master bedroom suite, a kitchen and dining area, as well as a two-car garage.

The theme of an eclectic assemblage of rooms of different periods and styles is established by the renovated and restored old rooms and continued into the new wing, where the interiors have been designed by the architect to have stylistic variety that encompass recent design modes.

The rooms from the demolished mansion, now included in this modern assemblage, were rooms bought in Europe and brought over by the original owner. It brings to mind René Clair's famous film entitled "The Ghost Goes West."

10 FEET

135

University Center, University of Michigan
Flint, Michigan 1980 – 1981

This center contains the non-academic campus activities, and is intended as the social focal point of a new campus. The building is organized and functions as a connecting link for pedestrian traffic moving from one end of the campus to the other. Internally, the activity spaces are organized off a circulation spine. Externally, the arrangement of the building volume is intended not only to provide a covered pedestrian way, but also to form the future outdoor gathering space on a growing campus. At the same time, the University Center defines the edge between the new campus and the Flint River, which is being cleaned up to become a green swath.

On the other hand, this new structure is intended as the formal entrance to the new campus.

The architecture thus employs a multiple-form system which encloses the new gathering space on the one hand and defines the campus's edge along the riverfront on the other. Program elements in the building are a rathskeller, an art gallery, a black-box theatre, a carpeted and sloped performance space, as well as a "leisure pool." In addition, the ground level contains a conference center. Second and third floors encompass a bookstore, a cafeteria, and dining **138** *spaces, as well as student organization offices.*

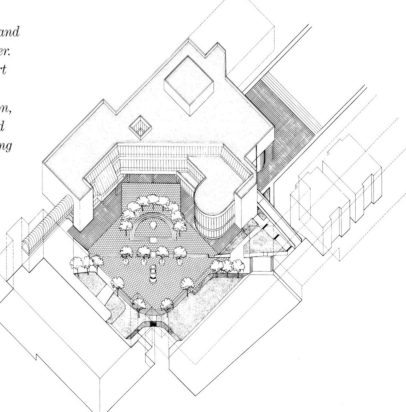

139

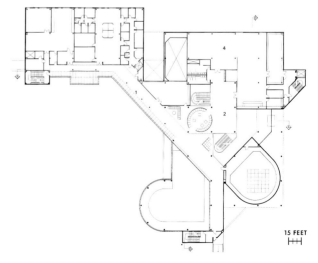

15 FEET

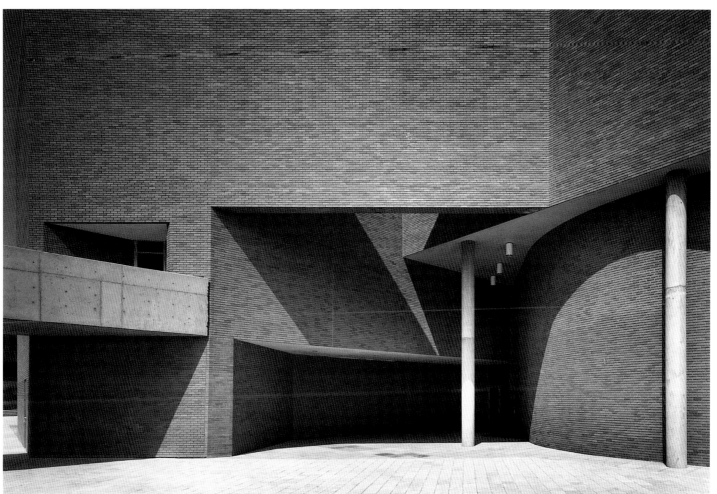

Boyce Thompson Institute, Cornell University
Ithaca, New York 1981

*The Boyce Thompson Institute is a private institution
for plant research now associated with the State College at
Cornell University.*

*The programmatic aspects of this building deal with two
very different building types. On the one hand there are
offices, a lecture hall, and library representing the
Institute's scholarly life; and on the other there are
the controlled environments, sealed biological laboratories,
as well as a plant culture wing, soil storage, potting room,
growth chambers, greenhouses, and extensive service
facilities.*

*The conceptual design of this building brings the two
programmatic elements together, grouped on either side
of a double-loaded corridor.*

*The element containing the scholars, their offices, and
graduate student spaces is located along the main campus
pedestrian route, providing a people-scaled aspect
to this side of the building.*

*The other element containing the sealed laboratories
requires 100 percent fresh air. In order to recapture heat
from the air being expelled, two enormous heat recovery
wheels have been mounted on the south side and give the
building the image of a giant machine.*

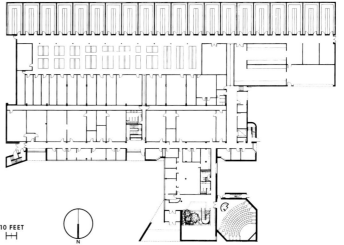

10 FEET

N

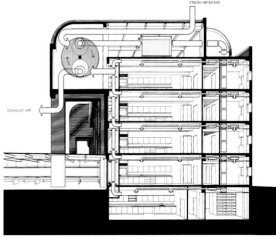

FRESH AIR INTAKE

EXHAUST AIR

Although Ulrich Franzen may be best known today for "collage architecture," several other interests have shaped his buildings at various times.

One of these was the recognition that movement, sometimes very rapid movement, makes us look at buildings (and at much else) in a very different way from the experience of people in earlier times. Such an obvious fact is nonetheless frequently overlooked; yet there is almost nothing in the human experience that changes our view of our environment as much as the experience of speed.

Painters and sculptors and, needless to say, photographers and filmmakers responded to that change from the very start of the twentieth century. But most architects, when asked to define movement through and among buildings, still seemed to think of it as little more than a fairly conventional, traditional, pedestrian progression.

Yet our current way of life is obviously quite different from what it was for our ancestors, before the invention of increasingly rapid moving vehicles, from automobiles to airplanes to interplanetary rocketry. We now see and experience objects (including buildings) in entirely different ways; and some of the architects of the late twentieth century, including Franzen, have understood that more clearly than others.

In 1971, Ulrich Franzen and several other architects were encouraged by the Ford Foundation to come up with radically new urban concepts that were not very likely to emerge from conventional architectural practice. Franzen's proposal was designed so it could, conceivably, be superimposed over the existing urban grid, and might, just possibly, see the light of day, some day.

Franzen presented his ideas in a film that showed Manhattan ringed by a highway system constructed above the waterways, and linked to the existing grid of streets on the island by elevated supply tubes and monorails that would bring in goods, services, and people, into whatever areas of the islands they inhabited, or worked in, or both. This system of supply tubes was further served by major warehouse areas located on the far sides of the rivers that ring Manhattan, in Queens, in Brooklyn, and in New Jersey. In the film, aerial views of Manhattan showed cars and buses zipping along on existing streets, interrupted only by traffic stops at intersections.

In the areas served by this superimposed urban machine, fossil-fueled vehicles would be banished and supplanted by electric pods for services and for personal transport. The streets would be liberated from massive traffic and pollution, and would offer space and light and air for a festive street life, uninterrupted by trucks and related noise, fumes, and other forms of unpleasantness. The object was to create a more humane and more livable city.

The film was really an abstraction of life in our cities as it presently seems to function, or might function in the future. The images were entertaining and memorable; they did not necessarily convey any solutions that would not be challenged by conventional planners. But unlike the images usually projected by such planners, Franzen's were imaginative and exciting: they suggested that a city, like Manhattan, could be viewed as a functioning machine, in which elements interacted efficiently and smoothly. And while there were certainly questions raised by Franzen's lively images, they seemed no more insoluble than those raised almost daily by the inefficiencies of existing urban situations.

But, most of all, the images showed a view of a modern city not often seen or presented by architects and planners. They were very different from the beautiful but static compositions of urban spaces that have been handed down

to us since the Renaissance. In short, Franzen was exploring an architecture for motion, rather than an architecture of static compositions.

Although he has not been able to translate all those filmed images into real urban spaces, Franzen did design and build a number of projects that convey the sense of an "architecture for motion" with admirable clarity. Admittedly, most of those projects were relatively small; but they were quite different from anything else being done at the time.

The most impressive project was his expansion of Hunter College, in Manhattan. When Franzen was retained to work on this project, the College consisted of a couple of buildings located, roughly, between Park and Lexington Avenues, along East 68th Street. The existing facilities were built for 2,300 students, and the expansion would enable the College to accept about five times that number, and would contain libraries, common rooms, athletic facilities, numerous new classrooms, faculty offices, and much more.

In a conventional institution, one would expect to find the same numbers of students and teachers, and the same number of facilities, housed on several dozen acres of land, and surrounded by much open space and other supporting facilities. Yet what Hunter College hoped to build was, in effect, an entire campus, on a site that was clearly too small to accommodate that kind of facility, and that was also bisected and trisected by very busy Manhattan streets and subways.

Obviously, none of this could be done by conventional means. And so Franzen explored a third and fourth dimension that might make it possible for the College to achieve what it wished to do. His solution was to construct two towers, each of them 17 stories tall, linked to each other by skywalks that crossed the adjacent streets and avenues at third and fifth floor levels. Moreover, the towers would be connected to an existing subway system that would bring in many of the students and faculty members, daily, without creating major traffic jams at street level. There would be a sunken, open-air pedestrian plaza, a sunken gymnasium or two, and various other facilities that would not interfere with existing traffic patterns at street or subway levels. Escalators would link all these facilities – and third floor skywalks would connect the towers to the old, existing Hunter College facilities.

To further complicate Franzen's job, the program envisaged by Hunter College would have to meet and satisfy an endless number of urban rules and regulations that would have to be amended in order to create as unorthodox an organism as he envisaged. There were, of course, the usual problems of designing and building for a college whose faculties, students, and administrators would probably find it difficult to arrive at a consensus on any plan, proposal, or (for that matter) on anything else. To advance a set of ideas as unconventional as those proposed by Franzen was a sure prescription for a nightmare, and he realized all that from the start.

For various political and budgetary reasons, the Hunter College plan advanced by Franzen was delayed, and it took more than ten years to complete the project, despite the great skills of the president of Hunter College, Dr. Jaqueline Wexler, a first-rate administrator and diplomat. She was an ideal client who finally managed to persuade all the various parties involved in this radical experiment to collaborate. The change in make-up of faculty and student bodies over so long a period of time makes the eventual completion of the Hunter College complex even more remarkable.

But, most of all, the nature of the new Hunter complex itself was highly innovative. Several other architects had, at various times, proposed three- and four-dimensional systems of urban connection; but except for a few

overpasses and underpasses between urban buildings, none had ever been successfully constructed in the U.S., and turned into coherent, urban organisms.
The Hunter College complex, when completed, did not seem radically innovative when seen from the street; but once inside one is immediately impressed by the dimensions and the inherent logic of this elevated campus, and the fun and excitement of moving around inside this urban machine.

Franzen was able to design and build several other structures that were conceived as "architecture for motion" rather than as single, static buildings. Invariably, these are buildings that would house several related, or sometimes contradictory functions – buildings that are, in effect, assemblages of several functions. The University Center at the University of Michigan, in Flint, is one such assemblage of half a dozen different buildings, a store, library, conference center, an auditorium (or two), a pool, a couple of dining rooms, and half a dozen other facilities, not necessarily related, and Franzen turned all this into a building that is a village, with an indoor commons, an outdoor court (or two), and several other facilities, all of which can be reached from a Main Street that connects everything and reaches out into minor facilities by means of "side streets."

It is, in short, not so much a building but an assemblage of facilities that add up to an "architecture in motion, though less complex and less difficult than the Franzen's design for Hunter College. Even some of his larger houses, like the Krauss Residence in Old Westbury, New York, which is really a collection of existing and added facilities, resemble nothing so much as small villages that seem to have sprung up around a main street, and suggest a busy traffic pattern around the clock.

To realize how radical all this must have seemed at the time, one should compare Franzen's "architecture for motion" with some of the static projects being built at the same time by other architects: Lincoln Center in Manhattan was completed at roughly the same time as the Hunter College campus. But at Lincoln Center the buildings are isolated events, barely relating to each other. There are virtually no connections above or, for that matter, below ground. There are no arcaded walkways to link the various concert halls and theatres – although it would have been easy to link them at various levels and greatly enhance pedestrian circulation. And only a minimal effort was made to link the new structures to mass transit lines or other traffic systems. In fact, except for the steel framing that holds up the Lincoln Center buildings, they could have been designed and built several hundred years earlier. Franzen's "architecture for motion", especially at Hunter College, was and is clearly a work of the twentieth century.

Shortly after completing his Hunter College campus, Franzen began work on what may be his most interesting "collage" building to date: the World Headquarters for the Philip Morris company.

Philip Morris had purchased some of the air rights over Grand Central Station, and proposed to build an executive office structure directly opposite the very imposing, Neoclassical building built by Warren & Wetmore between 1903 and 1913. A condition of the sale of air rights to the railroad was the establishment of rigorous guidelines and design controls that demanded a harmony in materials, scale, details, and facade elements between the new building and Grand Central Station, aspects that had little to do with the aesthetics of modern American architecture in the 1980s.

The first major, and entirely modern building designed by Ulrich Franzen and dominated by those concerns is the World Headquarters for the Philip Morris company, which was constructed between 1981 and 1984 in the center of Manhattan.

This building was largely shaped by extremely difficult and often contradictory demands and concerns. For example, as a result of the Philip Morris purchase of the air rights over Grand Central Station, the city's Landmarks Commission would exercise a high degree of design control over the new building.

These design controls applied especially to the north facade, which would face Grand Central Station. The east facade, which adjoins existing buildings along Park Avenue, was to relate primarily to the buildings along that avenue, and possibly to the side street (41st Street) on the south side of the block. The height of the new building, as well as certain setbacks and cornice lines, had to fit in as well. In short, the Philip Morris Building is a work of collage architecture, produced to satisfy a considerable number of guidelines laid down by the Landmarks Preservation Commission, as well as by Franzen's own concerns about context, spatial relationships, and urban cohesion.

It became a very unusual building in a different sense as well: because of Franzen's long interest in the other visual arts, he managed to persuade the Whitney Museum of American Art to establish an outpost on the ground floor of the Philip Morris Headquarters Building; and that branch museum, open to 42nd Street, is a very handsome, 30 feet tall space close to the Grand Central facades in scale.

The Whitney Museum outpost was such a success that Franzen was able to persuade the museum to establish a presence in a number of other commercial buildings as well. In each case, a portion of a building or building complex, easily accessible to the general public, would be turned into gallery space, and the Whitney would supply works of art to be exhibited there. The branch museum opposite Grand Central is the most prominent of these, but there would soon be others, both in New York City and in Connecticut, and other museums have been inspired to follow suit and to establish branches or outposts in many parts of the world.

The Philip Morris World Headquarters, with its very different and quite contradictory facades, may be the most prominent of Franzen's "collage" buildings.
But there are several others: "Multi-Cat" has already been mentioned; another one, technologically quite as interesting, is the Boyce Thompson Institute for plant research, also at Cornell, and built in 1981. The Institute is a huge, almost 400 feet long greenhouse on one side, as well as sealed laboratories and faculty offices on the other. (The laboratory and office part of the building is topped by an enormous heat recovery system – another structure that looks like a huge machine!) Still another "collage" building is the First City National Bank in Binghamton, New York. One side faces the street and addresses itself to the public and the town; another consists of terraces largely for the office staff and visitors, and faces the Chenango River and the spectacular view of its valley. In all of these buildings, the different aspects or programs of the buildings have suggested a different kind of facade; and Franzen responded to that notion instead of complying with some hard-and-fast architectural discipline.

The Philip Morris Headquarters is not only a work of collage architecture, but also a work of contextual architecture, though hardly a simplistic one. "The building is reticent and conservative in the choice of stone as an exterior finish. But in terms of compositional devices it is very avant-garde," Franzen says. "It became very controversial. The use of two different facade treatments was a way of clearly indicating that there are two very different urban situations, 42nd Street and Grand Central across the street, and Park Avenue, with all its big corporate headquarters standing there like a bunch of girls at a junior prom, waiting to be introduced. Creating two very different facades was also a way of making the building less conservative in its attitude, something not entirely proper." It is not clear whether Philip Morris, or the Landmarks Preservation Commission, realized that the architect was not being "entirely proper." Probably not.

The Evolving City, Project "Street"
Sponsors: The American Federation of the Arts and The Ford Foundation 1974

After studies lasting several years, a film was created illustrating new models for action in reorganizing the most densely populated areas of New York.

The aim was to reorder and re-apportion the public right-of-way by removing present service and transportation systems and replacing them. Not building but reordering.

The premises of our study were as follows:

• The crucial problem is the quality of life for residents and the integrity of the environment sustaining this life.

• The limits of man's ability to tolerate the man-made overloads in the scale of structures, population densities and urban support systems have been exceeded.

• A sense of place is a fundamental biological need contributing to human identity and dignity.

Man must maintain his roots in nature; therefore the elements of nature such as light, water, and vegetation must be accessible to him.

• The limited resources of the world demand an efficient reordering of all energy systems, if there is to be an acceptable future.

154 *The design, as well as the final form of the film, were intended to mobilize fresh thinking.*

156

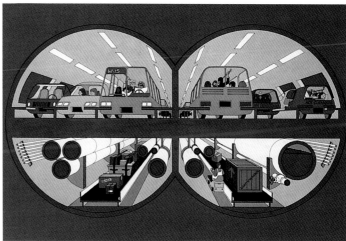

157

Hunter College
New York, New York 1975 – 1984

*The new Hunter College originated in the overcrowded
condition of the existing College originally built for 2,300
students but now serving nearly 10,000 students. A program
for new spaces was developed consisting of a gross area of
800,000 square feet encompassing everything from
competition gymnasiums to lecture halls and a new 500,000
volume library.*

*The architectural concept of this magnitude on an extremely
limited urban site dictated an unprecedented vertical
solution. The enormous foot traffic of up to 10,000 people
within this complex on an hourly basis suggested "skywalks"
to prevent intolerable congestion at street level and an eight-
story high escalator system integrated with elevators.*

*The expanded college consists of four very large buildings
making, in effect, a campus. However, unlike traditional
campuses, where more generous site areas permit open space
as the common ground, the site limitations brought about
another solution. Rather than an open-space commons, a
"main street" connecting all buildings at the third floor was
designed, crossing 67th Street as well as Lexington Avenue
in the form of skywalks. Along this third-floor street are
placed the entrance to the library, main cafeteria, snackbar,*

158 *as well as access to the escalator bank, tower elevator lobbies,
existing buildings, and lounges – all facilitating socializing
and a sense of place and community.*

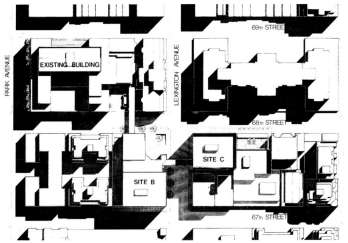

159

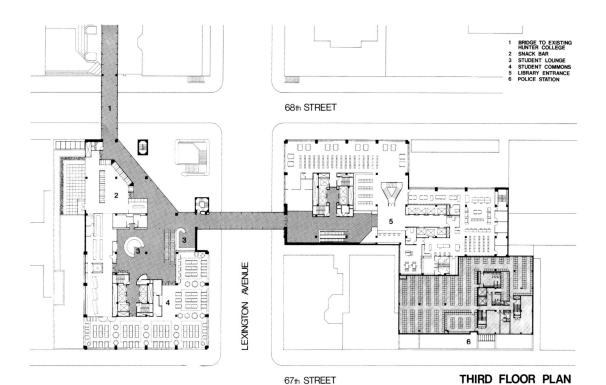

68th STREET

LEXINGTON AVENUE

67th STREET

THIRD FLOOR PLAN

160

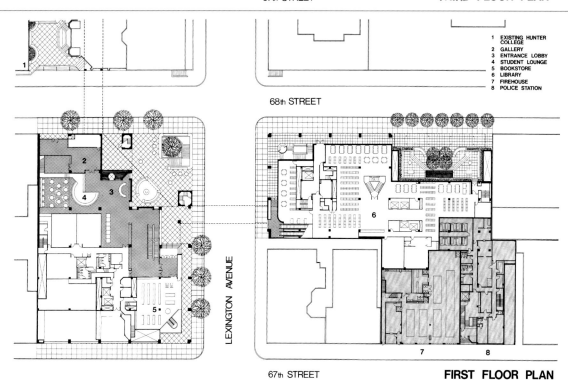

68th STREET

LEXINGTON AVENUE

67th STREET

FIRST FLOOR PLAN

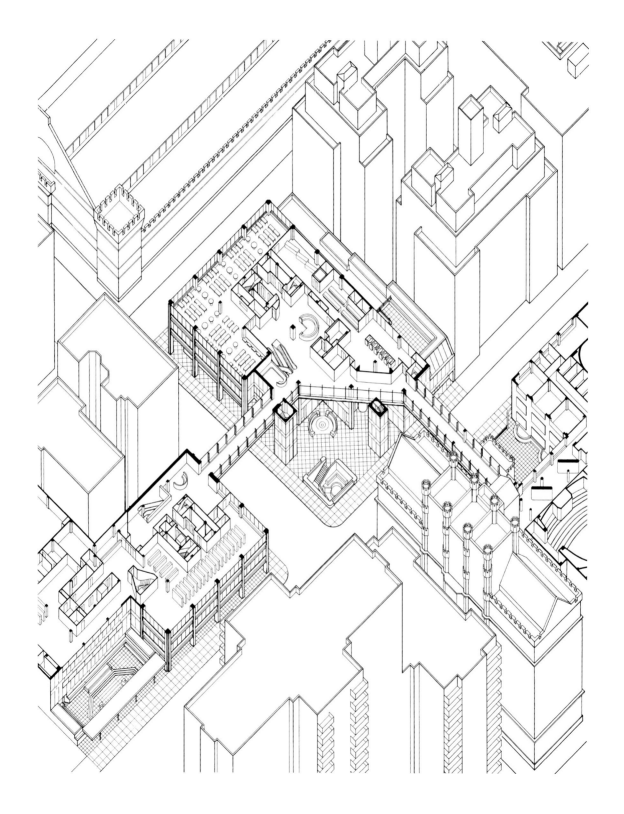

CIRCULATION

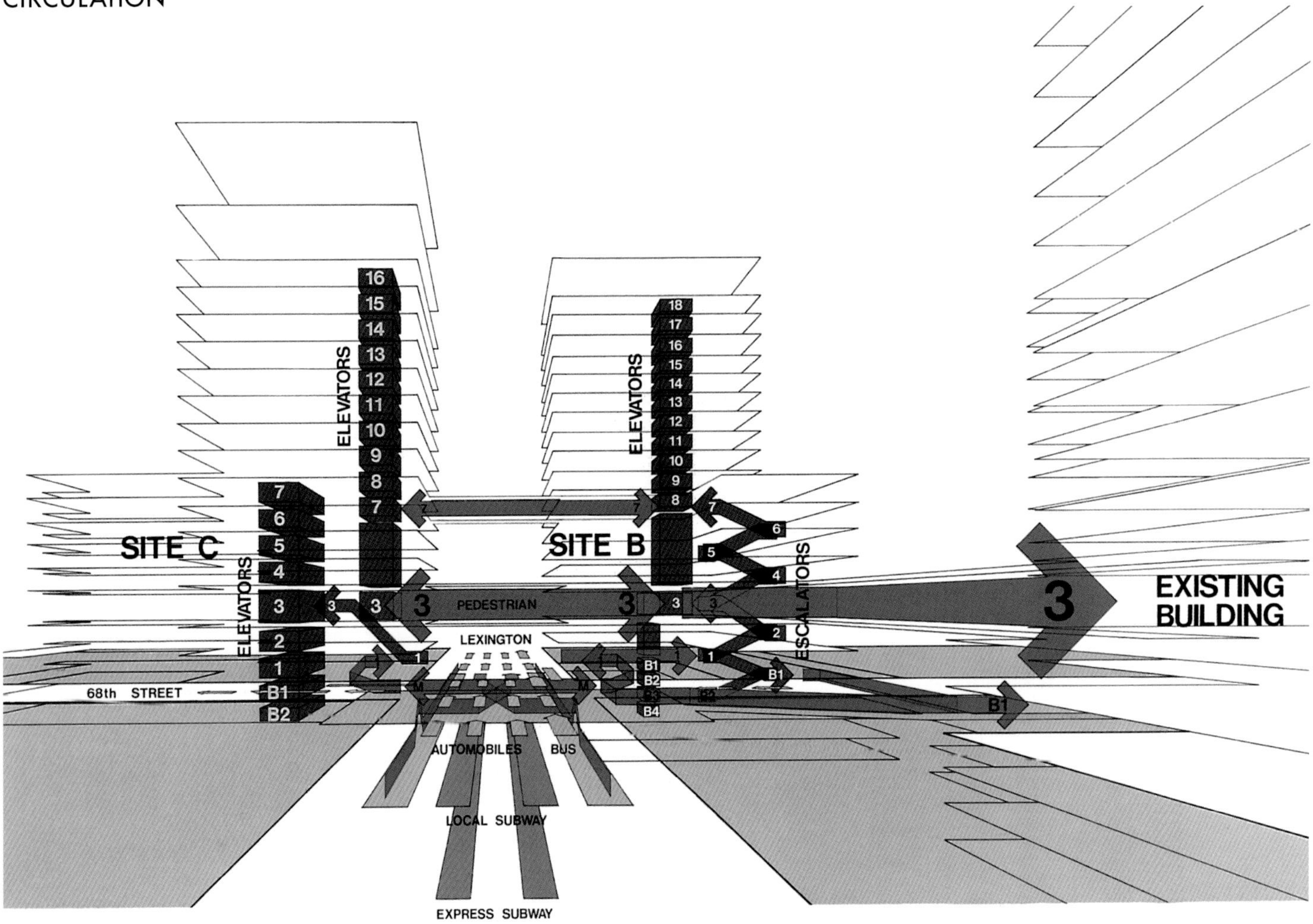

162

SITE C

SITE B

ELEVATORS

ELEVATORS

ELEVATORS

ESCALATORS

EXISTING
BUILDING

PEDESTRIAN

LEXINGTON

68th STREET

AUTOMOBILES   BUS

LOCAL SUBWAY

EXPRESS SUBWAY

163

165

Miller Brewing Company Visitors Centers
Various Locations 1980 – 1982

*Modern breweries are like huge food processing machines in
appearance rather than traditional breweries. Studies were
commissioned to explore two alternatives to the usual
walking visitors tour found in most breweries.*
*Two studies were commissioned: one study looked at the
possibilities of a visitors center as a monorail station. The
monorail was to give a ride through the plant and extensive
grounds. The other study proposed a visitors center building
with a viewing tower from which these enormous plants
could be observed.*

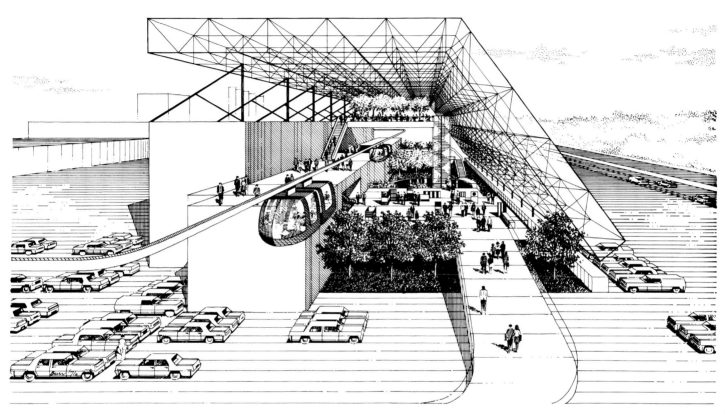

Champion International World Headquarters
Stamford, Connecticut 1984 – 1985

The project consists of a 15-story structure housing
Champion International's corporate offices,
an eight-level parking garage for 1,000 cars and a
public plaza.
Noteworthy are the fenestration employing various
arrangements of external louvers to reduce summer
sun-heat gain. The garage functions as a barrier from
the noise of the nearby turnpike and acts as a screen
for the plaza.
Major design concerns were to create a building strongly
oriented toward the general public and to form a gateway
into downtown Stamford.
The Champion Plaza is easily accessible to Champion
employees, as well as pedestrians. At the entrance to
the Plaza along Atlantic Avenue, a minimalist portal
was erected framing the landmarked Neoclassical
post office across the street. Thus the Plaza design
relates to the broader framework of the existing
community.
The extensive arcades forming sheltering sidewalks
along the main street, and especially the Whitney Branch
Museum adjoining the main lobby, offer significant
170 *amenities to the general public.*

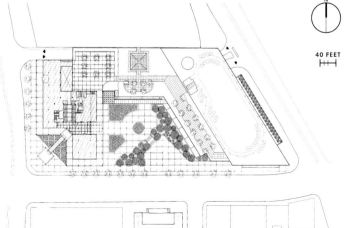

N

40 FEET

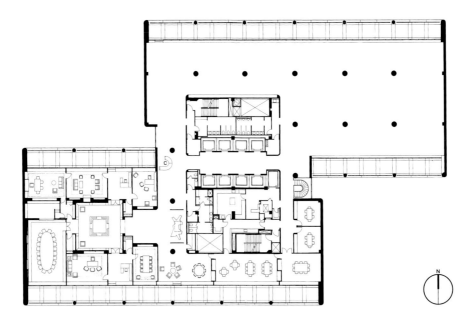

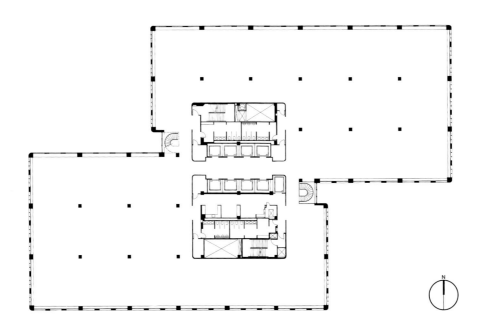

175

Philip Morris World Headquarters
New York, New York 1984

*The physical character of the Philip Morris building
is generated by the context of its setting.
To begin with, approval of the plans for this building by
the Landmarks Preservation Commission were required.
A pre-condition for a go-ahead was assurance of contextual
harmony with Grand Central Station, as well
as nearby buildings.
While the volumetric organization of the building
responds to a classic system, the facade treatments of the
building relate, on the one hand to the formal qualities
of Park Avenue, and on the other to the hustle and bustle
of 42nd Street.
The major thrust of the design are the lower four floors
which lie within the area of a pedestrian's perception.
These are designed as extensions of the sidewalk and the
street life by means of arcades, sheltered recesses,
and a new kind of museum with a covered sculpture park.
The enormous crowds that move past the building
on their daily trips to work from the station are here offered
a quiet respite from the city and the contemplative pleasure
that comes from works of art.*

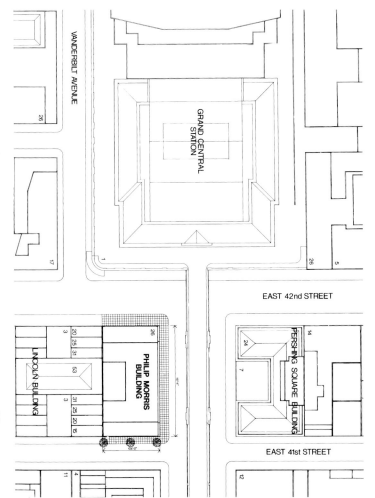

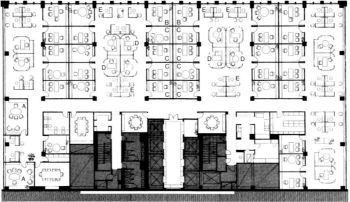

20 FEET

PARK AVENUE

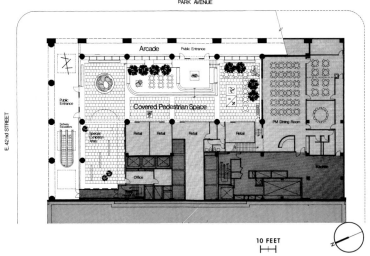

Arcade
Public Entrance

Public
Entrance

Covered Pedestrian Space

PM Dining Room

Special
Exhibition
Area

Retail Retail Retail Retail

Kitchen

Office

E. 42nd STREET

10 FEET

PARK AVENUE

Arcade

Open

PM Lobby

Vestibule

Lower Elevator Concourse

Open

E. 42nd STREET

E. 41st STREET

10 FEET

Morris House, Greenwich, Connecticut 1994

*The program for this substantial house was organized into
three wings so that the resultant building volumes would
still be domestic in scale.*

*The project is located on a parklike property overlooking a
small lake which became the focus of the plan organization.
As in some other residential projects, the lake view becomes
apparent here only after one enters the house.*

*The exterior of the house is a warm-toned and polished
concrete block revealing its aggregate as a texture. The
second story of the south wing is finished in a soft-toned
stucco above the cast stone to reduce its apparent bulk.*

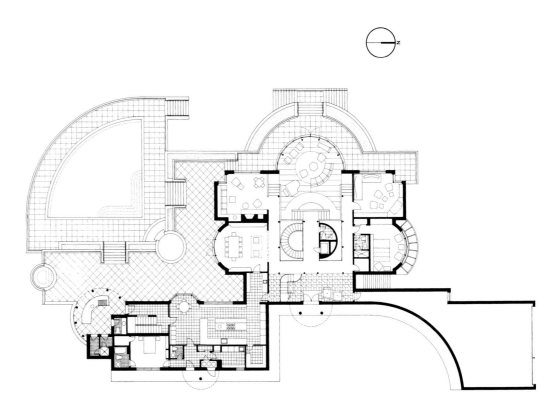

183

Millie and Arne Glimcher House
Long Island, New York 1985

This summer house was designed for a couple of serious collectors of modern art and their family. The site is fairly low land, of no particular topography, and paralleling a narrow pond in eastern Long Island. The house sits on a podium designed in part to serve as protection against occasional floods. The grounds serve as a setting for major modern works of sculpture. Exterior walls are of cast stone inside and out. The coloration and texture of the stone is close to limestone, the initially preferred material.

The house is organized around a central garden court which serves as the major socializing and circulation space. The central court is paved in a pattern of granite and marble. The interior of the glass vault above the garden court is equipped with a horizontal awning of white translucent cloth to screen the sun. Stylistic flourishes are kept to a minimum so as to provide a background of permanence. The two halves of the house separate the owner's bedroom suite from the loft-style bedrooms of two college-aged sons on the upper floor. On the ground floor, surrounding the garden court, lie the kitchen and dining area on the one hand, and on the other a den with a fireplace. The floor finishes of the two halves are of dark-stained oak and interior walls are covered with linen canvas and light-oak trim.

184

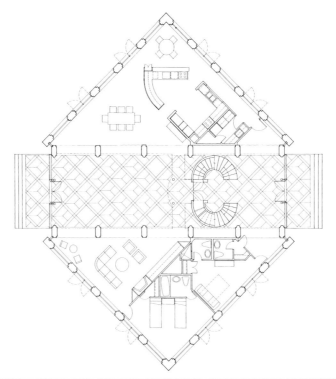

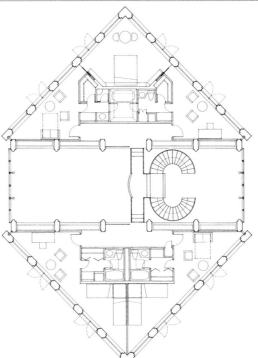

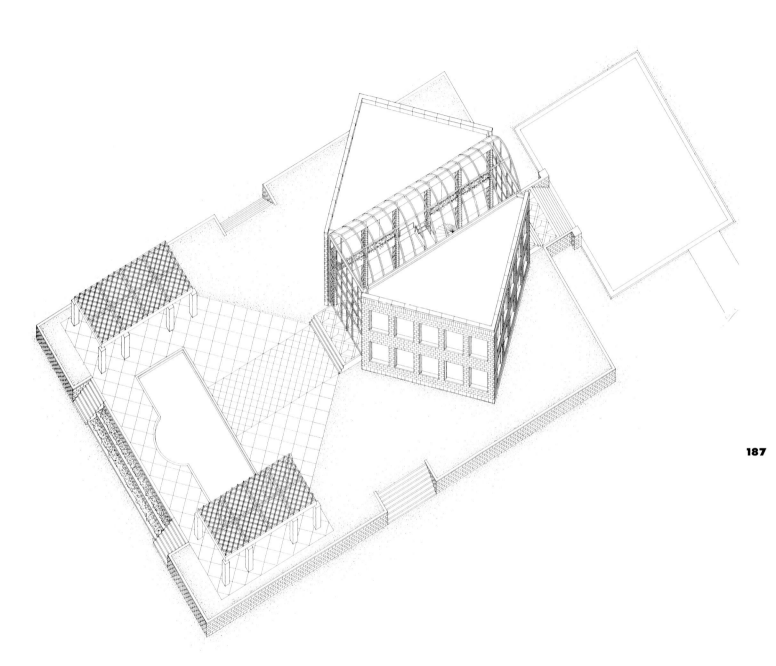

189

5

Many architects working during the past decades spent much of their time on projects that were never built, and Franzen is no exception. Although he completed an impressive number of important buildings, most of them still in excellent condition, some of his unbuilt projects are as impressive as those that were actually constructed.

Some of these were unsuccessful competition entries; others were never completed because the clients ran out of money. But a number of his unbuilt projects often conveyed ideas as convincing as some of the best buildings of their time.

The most interesting of Franzen's unbuilt projects, in all likelihood, was the 1969 Astor Place Building for Cooper Union, planned for a very complex corner site in Lower Manhattan. The site is more or less triangular, and it is contained between Fourth Avenue, Lafayette Street, Cooper Square, Astor Place, and several other projecting blocks that all converge, more or less, on the Cooper Union Foundation Building designed in the mid-nineteenth century by Fred Petersen. That building was and is a formal, Neoclassical structure with several innovative engineering features; to the north of the Foundation Building, an undistinguished "Engineering Building" was constructed in the 1960s; and to complicate things still further, a beautiful, Neoclassical Wanamaker Department Store, off Broadway, was severely damaged by fire in the 1950s, and subsequently demolished.

In designing what was going to be the New Astor Place Building, Franzen attempted to turn all these somewhat unrelated spaces, streets and adjacent buildings into a unified urban complex that would form a downtown campus. His proposal was probably the most challenging work of "collage architecture" he had attempted up to that point; indeed, it would have created one of the most remarkable urban focal points to be found in Manhattan, something on par with Times Square, Columbus Circle, or Madison Square Park, although not in dimensions. Alas, it was not to be. Perhaps Franzen's Astor Place will be realized some day, and the Cooper Union "campus" will then be one of the best triangulated landmark spaces in Manhattan.

He obviously saw his new Astor Place Building as a good deal more than a focal point at the intersection of two diagonal avenues. In Manhattan, most streets are parts of an enormous rectilinear grid, except where the streets are diagonal and intersect with the grid accordingly. At those intersections, buildings become wedge-like monuments that can then become significant and highly visible reference points. The Flatiron Building between Fifth Avenue and Broadway is one; the Times Tower and Duffy Square opposite the tower is another; and various triangular islands, parks, buildings, and circles are almost as visible. It was clear to Franzen that the Astor Place Building would be just as visible from a diagonal street, as the Flatiron Building would be from Madison Square, where Broadway and Fifth Avenue intersect.

So the approach to the north side of the new Cooper Union Building would be of major importance, and he shaped it so that a great loggia, in the Florentine manner, would face up Fourth Avenue and turn that side of the new building into a very visible entrance portico for a new Cooper Union campus. Although the grand portico would have been more symbolic than real, it would have seemed like a major entrance to the campus, and would have played down the significance of the unfortunate Engineering Building to the East.

Franzen's New Astor Place Building would have faced in several directions: to the east it would have faced the Cooper Union Foundation Building on Fourth Avenue; to the north, it would have faced up Fourth Avenue, as suggested earlier; and to the west it would have faced onto Lafayette Street, with its arcaded facades. In short, like other buildings done by Franzen during those years, the new Astor Place Building would have been another work of "collage architecture."

But more than anything else, the Astor Place Building would have been reminiscent of some of Le Corbusier's buildings, especially his monastery of La Tourette, a building quite far removed from the Miesian structures that used to influence Franzen's earlier buildings. Some day, perhaps, Franzen's building for Cooper Union will be built; it would become a major asset to a part of Lower Manhattan that is in need of that "simultaneous solution of opposites" that intrigued both Aalto and Le Corbusier, and it would significantly contribute to modern American architecture. In virtually all of his work, Ulrich Franzen seems to have tried to achieve that kind of "simultaneous solution of opposites," unquestionably the most difficult resolution to accomplish in architecture, or in any other art. In all of his work, especially in all of his recent work, Franzen has attempted to resolve inherently contradictory ideas and concerns.

I suggested at the start of this text that modern architecture, by the end of the twentieth century, had largely ceased to be an art and had become something of a business, an exercise in salesmanship; and that, as a result, much of our architecture had developed this deplorable flaw: bad taste. Many of Ulrich Franzen's contemporaries have done fairly well as salesmen, but not quite so well as artists. Franzen is one of the exceptions. As one of his contemporaries in architecture, I have long envied and admired him for his accomplishments in the areas that really determine the quality of buildings: accomplishments in theory, in technology, in imagination and, most of all, in art. The buildings described in this book are the work of a true artist in our field.

Astor Place Building for The Cooper Union, New York, New York 1969

The Cooper Union includes a school of engineering as well as a school of art and architecture. These departments are located in several buildings, with the historic landmark designed by Peter Cooper, and containing the library, the arts studios, as well as architecture spaces and administration. The Cooper Union has no identifiable center or campus. The brief for the new Astor Place Building envisaged it as the College Center. It was to include the library, a major dining facility, administration offices, as well as an art gallery and auditorium. Most importantly, all offices dealing with student life were to be concentrated here. The plans for the new building acknowledged its central purpose and location. The site just south of Astor Place and facing north up Fourth Avenue would create the opportunity for a major entrance to the institution. At the same time, by closing off Fourth Avenue between the historic Foundation Building and the new Campus Center, a small pedestrian campus would be created. In order to affirm this proposed campus, a way had to be found to extend its meaning from function and convenience to history. It was proposed that the statue of Peter Cooper presently standing at the southern end of the Foundation Building be moved to the new plaza to face north and overlook the new campus.

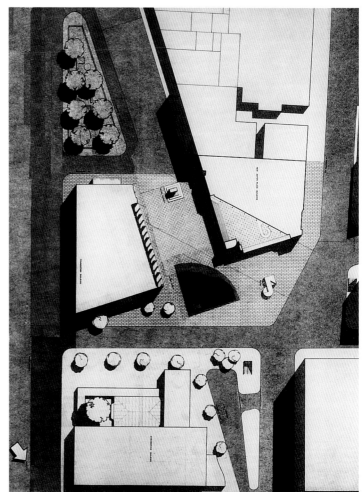

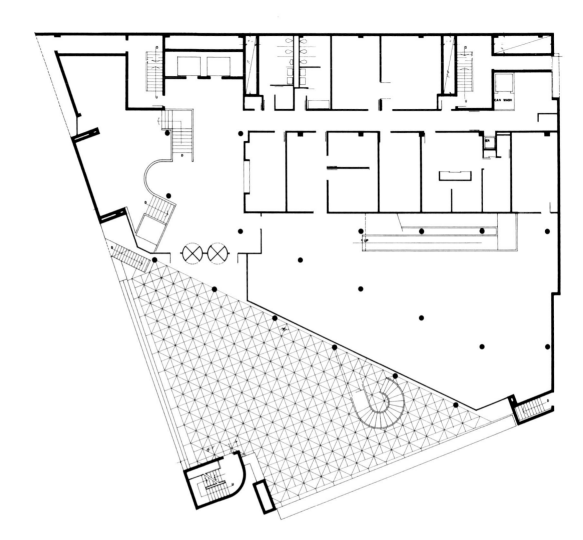

Associates and Architectural Staff
1958 – 1998

David Acheson
Scott Akins
Allen Anderson
Hobart Betts
Dennis Blackett
François Bollack
Les Brown
Richard Cook
Roger Diao
Nancy Freedman
Regi Goldberg
Nancy Goshow
Drew Greenwald
Mindi Greenwald
Charles Gwathmey
Eric Hoskinson
William Jacquette
Tom Joseph
John Kanastab
Jan Kangro
Bill King
Rod Knox
Etel Kramer
Eugene Kremer
Keith Kroeger
Tunny Lee
Steven Lewent
Dimon Liu
Philip Logan
Zack McKown
Gerald Nyberg
Samuel Nylen
Terry O'Neill
Leonard Perfido
James S. Polshek
Jim Rhodes
Edward Rosen
Dani Rosen
Robert Scarpa

Barbara Stauffacher
Tom Thornton
Paul Weissman
Vernon West
Ives Zimmerman